BUDDHA, MARX, AND GOD

PROPHETIC RELIGION

BUDDHA, MARX,
AND GOD

Some aspects of religion in the modern world

TREVOR LING

LECTURER IN COMPARATIVE RELIGION
IN THE UNIVERSITY OF LEEDS

MACMILLAN
London · Melbourne · Toronto

ST MARTIN'S PRESS
New York
1966

MACMILLAN AND COMPANY LIMITED
Little Essex Street London WC 2
also Bombay Calcutta Madras Melbourne

THE MACMILLAN COMPANY OF CANADA LIMITED
70 Bond Street Toronto 2

ST MARTIN'S PRESS INC
175 Fifth Avenue New York NY 10010

Library of Congress catalog card no. 67–10332

PRINTED IN GREAT BRITAIN

CONTENTS

Contents

Buddhism and community. The community's central concern. The community and secular society.

Contents

development in Islam and Communism. Islam, Communism, and religious practice. Materialism: ideological versus pragmatic.

IV: Theology and Religion

ACKNOWLEDGEMENTS

In the following chapters use has been made of certain passages which have already appeared in *The Hibbert Journal*, *The Church Quarterly Review*, *The Middle Way*, and *Mikkyo Bunka* (Koya-san University, Japan), and a talk in the Third Network of the B.B.C. Sincere thanks are due to those concerned for permission to reproduce this material.

PREFACE

This book is intended for those who are in any way interested in the subject of religion in the modern world. Unlike Henry Fielding's hero, when I say religion I do not mean only the Christian religion, much less the Protestant form of it practised in this country. Even in Britain it is both archaic and parochial in the extreme to assume that 'religion' means Christianity. The study of religion refers, as Ronald Hepburn has recently said,[1] to a whole range of human activities, not simply Western theistic ones. Nevertheless one sometimes even now encounters the attitude among Christian theologians that all other religious traditions are not worth consideration, practised as they are by 'less advanced' peoples in remote parts of the earth (from Britain), and characterized by the use of strange and slightly ridiculous Indian or Arabic, Chinese or Japanese terminology; all this, it is hinted, is no fit subject for civilized Christians to waste their time upon.

Happily, however, this attitude tends to be confined to the more conservative professional theologians. Sociologists, historians and geographers certainly have broader horizons. And so, in general, have the reading public, who seem to be more aware of the fact that we live in a religiously pluralistic world.

Again, a modern history and philosophy of religion, if it is to be distinguishable from the old 'natural theology' of Christian scholasticism, with its logical arguments for the existence of God, must be concerned with the empirical study of religion in the very wide range of its manifestations. What I have attempted to do here is to examine the religious aspect of human affairs in two or three of its major forms. Examined

[1] *Religion and Humanism* (1964), p. 90.

xi

thus, however, in connection especially with Buddhism on the one hand, and Marxism on the other, and Western religion in the light of both, the investigation has led me into realms which may sometimes seem rather far removed from what are usually regarded in the West as the proper concerns of religious studies, in particular, into 'secular' history, politics, economics and sociology. But this only emphasizes that religion is a phenomenon having much wider associations than the somewhat reduced Western view of it sometimes allows.

In other respects the scope of the present study is severely limited. Philosophical problems are not among the major concerns here. For instance, in dealing with Buddhism, I have not attempted to go into the more profound questions dealt with in Buddhist philosophy; for this kind of approach to the subject the reader will need to turn to the recent work of such writers as T. R. V. Murti, Edward Conze, K. N. Jayatilleke and Ninian Smart. I have been concerned rather to show the way in which Buddhism presents itself to us as a *religious* tradition; how it stands in relation to secularism and Marxism; whether the latter is or is not to be regarded as a religion; and how, as a religion, Buddhism may possibly provide a corrective to any view of religion which is based only on its Western manifestations.

I should like to acknowledge the very valuable assistance, most readily given, of three colleagues in particular: Dr. A. P. M. Coxon of the Department of Social Studies; Dr. J. Ch'en of the School of History; and Mr. M. Milligan of the Department of Philosophy; all of whom have read and commented on sections of my typescript. I should also like to thank the staff of the Brotherton Library for their helpful assistance on many occasions, and Miss A. Ogden, Miss D. Raper and Miss M. Ward for their help in typing.

Leeds University   T. L.
January 1966

Part One

SECULARISM
AND
RELIGION

1

THE FUTURE OF RELIGION

THE BUDDHIST MONK AND THE DIESEL TRAIN

AMONG the writer's collection of colour-photographs taken in Burma in the early sixties is one which shows a Buddhist *phongyi*, or monk, in his saffron-coloured robe, standing on the platform of a railway station on the outskirts of Rangoon beside one of the modern blue-painted diesel trains made in Japan and supplied to Burma as part of Japanese war-reparations. Here, symbolically, are the ancient and the modern in juxtaposition: on the one hand, the monk in the simple robe that was worn by the holy men of India more than two thousand years ago, and on the other the diesel, the product of the highly complex industrial civilization of the twentieth century and a symbol of the rapid post-war recovery and westernization of the Japanese people. Burma and Japan are both Asian countries, and in both Buddhism has been an important element in the nation's life. If one were to ask which of these two countries represents the more important trends in the contemporary world, many people would probably say Japan. The Burmese Buddhist monastery and the Japanese factory — one wonders what possible connection there could be between these two, or, to speak more generally, between the Buddhist system of religion and the complicated technological society of the latter half of the twentieth century.

The religion of the Buddha may indeed seem at first somewhat archaic in comparison with the civilization whose symbols are the computer and the space ship. Moreover, looking back as it does to the ancient places of India and Ceylon, to Magadha and Gaya, Sarnātha and Anurādapura, Buddhism may also seem remote and alien from Western civilization, whose roots — historically at least — are in Athens and Jerusalem, and whose most representative cities now are Chicago and New York. Yet the possibility of a significant and vital relationship between Buddhism and the modern world is considerably greater than might be supposed. In order to demonstrate this it is necessary first to consider some general aspects of Western technological civilization.

The ordinary man of the twentieth century lives in a world and a climate of thought which in many ways is far removed from that of all the preceding centuries of history. The ordinary European of the early nineteenth century, for instance, had a great deal in common with the men of the tenth century, or even of the first, in his assumptions about human life and its place in the universe, about the nature of the physical world and the process of the human mind. The twentieth century has witnessed such radical changes in Europe and America that revolution is not too strong a word to describe what has taken place.

But a revolution is usually preceded by a period of ferment and growth of the forces that eventually show themselves in revolutionary form. The materialistic values which are characteristic of Western society today are not in themselves new; technological advances have simply brought them out more clearly into the open. They are manifest in the democracies of

the West in the dominance of money and the universal acceptance of hedonistic aims. The consumption of 'goods' is the
purpose of life. It is assumed that all men everywhere will
engage in the pursuit of material, largely physical, satisfactions,
notably more lavish and exciting foodstuffs, alcohol, tobacco,
and various other drugs. This is the basic assumption of the
commercial advertising which more and more dominates
Western society.

THE SICKNESS OF WESTERN SOCIETY

In his book *The Sane Society* Erich Fromm raises the important
question whether the people of the Western countries in the mid-
twentieth century can now really be said to be sane. He points
to some of the facts, aware that he is stating what have become
truisms. In the West we have, for example, created enormous
material wealth and we have also killed off millions of human
beings in periodic outbursts of mass violence which we dignify
by the name of war. The enemies of one year — 'cruel, irrational
fiends whom one must defeat to save the world from evil' are
our friends a year or so later, and those nations who were
previously our allies have now become our enemies. It is almost
superfluous to mention the follies of the economic 'system',
where a particularly bountiful crop is an economic disaster, and
where, although there are millions who need what we have in
abundance, we restrict productivity 'to stabilize the market'. In
connection with the popular 'culture' of a society in which
90 per cent of the population are literate he points out that radio,
television, movies, and newspapers are largely media to 'fill the
minds of men with the cheapest trash, lacking in any sense of
reality, with sadistic phantasies which a halfway cultured
person would be embarrassed to entertain even once in a
while'. To a prodigious extent time is saved by the most

ingenious of gadgets only to have to be 'killed' in some new way.

This is a society which claims to be sane. Yet this, and other more detailed information which we possess about such matters as suicide, homicide, and alcoholism, seem to indicate pretty clearly a society which is sick. Increasing affluence is accompanied by increasing numbers of alcoholics and suicides. The countries with the worst records with regard to both suicide and alcoholism are the U.S.A., Denmark, Switzerland and Sweden; in other words they are the countries which are 'the most democratic, peaceful and prosperous'.[1] Fromm concludes that the United States, which is the most prosperous and materially the most advanced, shows the greatest degree of mental unbalance.[2]

Moreover, where the United States leads, the rest of the Western world is following, as fast as it can. Nor is there much to choose in this respect between American capitalism and Russian communism; both have as their goal an 'ever increasing economic efficiency and wealth', both are 'societies run by a managerial class and by professional politicians'; both have a materialistic outlook, and 'both systems tend to converge'.[3]

Assuming that world war is avoided, Fromm sees the greatest danger facing mankind as that of becoming robots. The only likelihood that such robots will rebel is when, no longer able to stand the boredom of their totally meaningless life, they destroy their world and themselves.

The view of Western society which is presented here is doubtless in some respects over-simplified and could be significantly modified by the admission of other relevant considerations. A great deal of Fromm's picture of an insane society relates more particularly to the United States than to European

[1] Fromm, op. cit., p. 10.   [2] Ibid.   [3] Op. cit., pp. 358 f.

countries. But the social trend in the latter is towards the American situation. The difference is largely that America has arrived at this condition a few decades earlier. In broad outline the description which Fromm provides corresponds pretty closely to the kind of impression made by Western civilization upon the Asian visitor. Fromm's indictment of it is by no means uncommon, and is from time to time voiced by others — at least within the non-communist countries.

For the student of religion there are two immediate points of concern in the trend towards this kind of society. First, how will the religious cultures of Asia stand up to this trend? Will they succumb, or will they prove more resistant than the West? Second, what spiritual resources are there in the traditional religions of the East for dealing critically and constructively with this drift towards collective insanity? The concern of the first part of this book will be to consider how far Buddhist countries in particular are faring in their encounter with Western materialism, whether of the Marxist or non-Marxist variety; and what implications this may have for religion in the West.

Burma, for instance, is a country very much in transition from old to new. The effect of growing secularism is seen among university students at Rangoon, who, coming from traditionally Buddhist homes, tend to react against the religion in which they have been brought up when they begin to feel the impact of modern ways of thought and modern technology. They no longer keep the holy days, they no longer visit the pagoda regularly to pay homage to the Buddha, they no longer join in the daily chanting of sacred verses. This is, of course, a common reaction to childhood religion among students everywhere, but circumstances have combined in Burma, as in some other Buddhist countries, to make it particularly severe. Yet on the other hand (and this is the important

7

point to note), the same conditions which are weakening popular traditional beliefs and forms are also stimulating Burmese Buddhism to produce from within its own tradition something which is coming to be greatly valued by men living in a modern secularized society — the discipline and practice of Buddhist meditation. The recent growth of lay meditation-centres around the city of Rangoon is ample evidence of this. Those who resort to these centres are often the busiest of men, government officials and army officers and university teachers, who, in the increasingly secular context of their work and under its unrelenting pressures, have come to interpret their need in terms of the central religious practice of the classical Buddhism of the monasteries.

It is hardly necessary to point to the similar growth in popularity of retreat centres which is a feature of the contemporary religious life of the West. The two trends are not unrelated. Similar causes are producing a similar awareness in East and West of the need for the more searching disciplines of religion. The acids of modernity, while they may corrode some religious forms and beliefs which have outlived their usefulness, may also lay bare what is most precious in the great systems of religion. And in this process it is possible that one form of religious belief and practice may be modified by reference to another, as it sees where its own weaknesses in the encounter with modern secularism can be remedied by acknowledging the strength of other forms, manifested in the same encounter.

Probably the question to ask therefore is not: Will religion survive the modern encounter with secularism? but rather, *What kind* of religion will be most likely to emerge from the encounter? I believe that it can be very helpful to ask this question with reference to Buddhism, because on the one hand this is a form of religion which is considered by some to be more compatible with the modern secular climate than most other religions, and because on the other hand the kind of modification of its thought to which Buddhism may be challenged by the encounter with secularism is, I believe, likely to be of considerable significance to others besides Buddhists.

THE NEW REFORMATION

Buddhism is of some importance to anyone concerned with the religious situation in the West in another connection. It is said that the significant Christian response to the challenge of secular thought is already to be seen in the ferment which surrounds the names of Bultmann and Bonhoeffer, and that there is much in the contemporary Christian situation which suggests a new Reformation. It is claimed that the radical renewal of religious thought and practice which is beginning to emerge in response to twentieth-century scientific thought and technological culture is comparable to that earlier renewal which was associated with the Renaissance. This newly emerging religious radicalism may be in fact a great deal more radical than that of the Reformation, and may eventually have to be regarded as not only different in degree but different in kind from the religion out of which it will have emerged. This may be seen by the historian of religion to be only an intensification of a process of change and renewal which has been going on throughout the history of most of the living religions of the world. Seldom does a religion remain the same over a long period, if it is a living religion. The present renewal may therefore be taken as a sign that the religious tradition of the West is alive, and not moribund.

The present renewal has two aspects. There is a questioning of religious *practice* on the one hand — that is, it is being questioned how far religious practice of any kind is relevant in the modern world. On the other hand there is a questioning of the *theological forms* in which faith expresses itself. The study of Buddhist religious tradition has a certain relevance with regard to both of these.

Religion is notoriously difficult to define but, in the phrase 'religionless Christianity', what is meant is clearly the whole range of what are often called 'sacramentals': rites, ceremonies, festivals, holy days, holy places, myth and symbol, and even, if the idea be carried to its logical conclusion, sacred scriptures as well. In the twentieth century, it is said, religious activities and forms of this kind must inevitably wither away (for all really modern men, at any rate), and it is to this kind of situation that we must now address ourselves. The prospect which we are invited to consider is one in which Christian faith must find expression in ways that have hitherto been regarded as wholly secular, and *only* in these ways; especially, perhaps in some form of existentialism. Linked with this train of thought there is another: that any serious study of the great religions and their relation to Christ has now become an anachronism.

A great deal of the present discussion on this subject was, of course, sparked off by the writings of Dietrich Bonhoeffer, who, as Daniel Jenkins has pointed out, was greatly influenced by Barth, and developed his ideas out of Barthian theology by a train of thought which can be easily followed.[1] In a passage which has become a *locus classicus* in this connection[2] Bonhoeffer pointed out that Christian preaching and theology throughout its history had rested on the 'religious premiss' of man. He then went on to ask, 'But if one day it becomes apparent that this *a priori* "premiss" does not exist, but was an historical and temporary form of human self-expression ... what does that mean for Christianity?' It would mean, he suggested, the removal of the linchpin which held together the

[1] D. Jenkins, *Beyond Religion* (London, 1962), pp. 12, 23 ff.
[2] *Letters and Papers from Prison* (London, 1953), pp. 122 f.

whole structure of Christianity; for the problem would then be 'How can Christ become the Lord even of those with no religion?'

What is insufficiently considered by those who are now eager to embrace the idea of a religionless Christianity is Bonhoeffer's basic condition in this passage; 'if it becomes apparent' that the religious premiss does not exist. The question to be answered first is whether this has become apparent. Of course it is true that 'men with no religion' are to be found within modern society. Karl Heim describes such a man; he is the sophisticated secularist, who sees no need to find a meaning in life, who feels no guilt, no problem of evil, who knows that he will die and accepts the fact with a shrug, or with calm resignation, and has no ultimate concern whatever.

Further reflection suggests that this type of *individual* is no new creation of the technological age. He is not necessarily the newly-emerging prototype of the twenty-first century. He is probably as old as religion itself. The Psalmist knew of his existence. In ancient India he was called by Buddhists *akriya-vādin* (literally, he who says there is no [moral] result of action) and among the basically religious philosophies of India there was one distinguished from the others by its irreligiousness, namely, that of the *Cārvākas*, or materialists. Such men were probably not uncommon, either, in what are thought of now as the great ages of faith. In reading Shakespeare one has the impression that this kind of individual was a recognizable type even in Elizabethan England, that most religiously preoccupied age.

What we have not yet seen is an *entire society* from which all traces of religious consciousness have disappeared. We do not know, therefore, how stable such a condition would be, or whether the religious consciousness would not inevitably manifest itself in such a society in a new form. We have, in the twentieth century, seen a State with massive powers of coercion at its disposal which has *tried* to eliminate religion, but as yet without success. Walter Kolarz, in his recent study, *Religion in the Soviet Union*, comes to the conclusion that, far from withering away, religion in Russia is likely to outlive the present political system. If the total disappearance of religion were possible at all, there is no reason why it should have been delayed until now. There have been other ages in which it might have disappeared. To hold that this distinction is reserved for the twentieth century is to have too exaggerated an opinion of the sophistication (or the decadence) of our own age, compared with that, let us say, of classical Greece.

What is happening to religion in many parts of the world today is what has happened before, namely a refashioning of its forms, and a reorientation of its ideas. Mircea Eliade has drawn attention to certain elements of contemporary life where new forms of religious mythology and symbolism are taking the place of old ones. He has shown, for example, how the human mind cannot dispense with myth in some form, and has traced some of the ways in which the archetypal myths of religion must somehow find expression in some new religious form, albeit disguised as a kind of secularism. This, and similar work in the field of the psychology of religion, indicates the deep roots of the religious impulse in man. Perhaps the anthropologist R. R. Marett was not so far wrong when he claimed that the designation of man as *homo sapiens* might well be changed to *homo religiosus*. Nor should this be more than the Christian implies when he asserts that man is made in the image of God and that God is always seeking to make himself known to men. Failure to see an abiding significance in the whole area of human activity which is called religion, is, like the failure to recognize value in non-Christian aspirations towards God, as M. Jacques Cuttat has said, 'less a product of deep faith than of value-blindness with regard to the universal dimensions of Christ'.

All this suggests that the important question is not whether religion is about to disappear altogether, and if so, what will this mean for Christianity; but rather, what new forms religion is likely to take in the immediate future, in Asia, in Africa, in the West, and how these will concern the Church. This will mean that Christians have still as great an obligation as ever to consider the relationship between the Church and the whole non-Christian religious life of man. What is technically called 'the study of religion' remains highly relevant today, if by this we understand a study of how religions have developed in the past, how they are developing now, and how they are likely to develop in the immediate future. This is especially true in the case of Buddhism when it is considered as a religion, and this will be an important concern in subsequent chapters.

There is, however, another and rather different reason for concerning ourselves with Buddhism, namely, the increasing attraction felt in the West for Buddhist *thought*. This has relevance to the second aspect of the present religious renewal which is going on: the reshaping of theology, or the attempt to re-express essential Christian insight in terms of the present total situation, religious and secular. In certain respects the 'new theology' might be interpreted as an approximation to a Buddhist *type* of theology. It is most important that conservative Christian theologians — and others who think as they do — should not assume that this means a *reduced* theology, a theology which has sold the pass to the rationalist or to the secular humanist. One has at least to consider the possibility that this could mean the revitalizing of Christian thought. The plain evidence of the contemporary situation is that in modern Western society many are not convinced of the relevance of traditional Christian teaching, in spite of the massive advantages which traditional Christianity enjoys in the media of communication at its disposal. If, in the face of all this, there is a growing number of people who find more relevance in other traditions of thought, then conservative Christians should seek seriously to understand why this is so, and not attribute it entirely to the wickedness or stupidity of those to whom traditional Christian theology no longer appeals.

2

THE CONTEMPORARY APPEAL

OF BUDDHISM

BUDDHISM AND THE WEST

AT a Buddhist monastery near Rangoon, in 1961, I was introduced to a monk who had recently arrived there. At first sight he looked like any of the other monks of that country, with shaven head, orange robe, and bare feet. But he had, I noticed, a somewhat lighter skin than most, and spoke English more colloquially than is usual even among Western educated Burmans. He was, in fact, an Englishman who had resigned from a post in the Foreign Office in London to become a monk. As a child he had been brought up in one of the stricter Protestant sects. In his teens he had reacted to this by becoming an atheist. After some years of spiritual wandering he had come into contact with Buddhism in London, and had found in it a form of spirituality which seemed to meet his need. Now, through his experience of Buddhism and Buddhist meditation, he was coming to appreciate, in a way that had not been possible before, the spiritual tradition of Catholic Christianity. He had, he said, been deeply moved by reading the life of St. Teresa of Lisieux, and was turning once again to a study of the Fourth Gospel.

I use this man's story here as an illustration of the greatly increased possibility which exists nowadays in the West for a person to come into contact with an Eastern faith. In my own undergraduate days, just after the Second World War, there was no Buddhist Society at Oxford. There is one now, and it consists largely of British students who are interested in Buddhism, and not, as might have been supposed, of Asian nationals studying in this country. Similar societies have sprung up in the last few years in other universities and towns in Britain.[1] In the United States the growth of interest in eastern faiths is notorious, but it is by no means all of the rather sensational kind which one associates with California, beatniks and Zen.

The English Buddhist monk in Burma illustrates something peculiar to the present generation. Youthful reaction to an inadequately understood Christianity, a reaction which leads a young man to declare himself an atheist, is not unusual. What is relatively unusual, or has been until now, is for the same man to find his way back to a religious view of life, and to an appreciation of the spiritual treasures of his native heritage, through contact with an alien faith. This kind of experience may well become more and more common.

Moreover there are those Western-educated men of Asia who find themselves in the same position of religious scepticism. It is significant that the first Prime Minister of India, Pandit Nehru, a Hindu Brahman, schooled in Natural Science at Cambridge, and known throughout his life as an agnostic, is reported to have said during the latter years of his life that the one form of religion which attracted him was Buddhism.

[1] The latest of these, at the time of writing, was at the Imperial College of Science and Technology, London University.

16

The Contemporary Appeal of Buddhism

A FAITH FOR SPIRITUAL REFUGEES

According to Mr. Christmas Humphreys, Buddhism 'appeals to the West because it has no dogmas, satisfies the reason and the heart alike, insists on self-reliance coupled with tolerance for other points of view, embraces science, religion, philosophy, psychology, ethics and art, and points to man alone as the creator of his present life and sole designer of his destiny'.[1]

It would be unwise for the exponent of Buddhism to dwell too much on the statement that this is a religion which has no dogmas. The practice of Buddhism in Asia by lay people, and their respect for the Sangha, or order of monks, rests firmly on the acceptance of the principle of rebirth continuing through many human existences. Such belief may not be dogmatic in the sense of being laid down by an ecclesiastical authority, but it is the kind of belief whose truth or untruth is not demonstrable with any certainty and in this sense it is no less a dogma than Jewish, Christian, or Muslim belief in God. Moreover Buddhism has its authoritative doctrinal tenets; only it does not call them so — it calls them 'Holy Truths'. These come to men on the authority of the Buddha, and must first be accepted in faith, even though it is claimed that they may later be verified in personal experience. We shall be more fully concerned with this aspect of Buddhism in a later chapter.[2]

However, there are undoubtedly a number of reasons why modern man in search of a faith may find Buddhism attractive. The contemporary world is full of refugees of one kind and another. There are those who are actually in a physical sense refugees; but there are also those who in a spiritual sense have been uprooted or dispossessed in the clash of religious doctrines

[1] *Buddhism* (Penguin Books, 1951), p. 76.
[2] See Chapter 3.

with biological, psychological, or sociological ideas. Some are refugees from the problems raised by belief in God — whether by this we mean belief in God as a being who is at once omnipotent, benevolent, and just, or belief in God in any sense at all. The difficulties raised by the attempt to combine belief in God's omnipotence with belief in his benevolence and his justice are the classical ones that theodicy is concerned with. But more acute in our day for many people is the difficulty of believing in any sense in what they would call a *personal* supreme being. To those who find themselves in this situation, unable to believe in a personal God, yet conscious of a continuing need for some sort of transcendental reference for human life, for a system of morality and a spiritual discipline, Buddhism may appear to be exactly what they are seeking.

Others may be refugees from what they regard as the evils of ecclesiasticism. In spite of the demand which Buddhism makes for initial assent to certain propositions, there is an apparent absence of ecclesiastical and hierarchical authority in matters of belief, and this is a feature which counts strongly in Buddhism's favour in the eyes of some spiritual wanderers. In Buddhism there are no priests; no one pontificates; and there are no ecclesiastical sanctions of any kind — for the layman at least. The assent which has to be given, largely on trust, to certain moral and metaphysical propositions, is intended to serve only as the necessary preliminary to one's proving their truth for oneself at a later stage. These propositions, it is claimed, are grounded in the fact that the universe is the expression of certain laws. 'All effects have causes, and man's soul or character is the sum total of his previous thoughts and acts. Karma, meaning action-reaction, governs all existence, and man is the sole creator of his circumstances and his reaction to them, his future condition, and his final destiny.'[1] This seems to har-

[1] Christmas Humphreys, *Buddhism*, p. 74.

monise well with what many people believe to be modern scientific thought.

Others again are refugees from that kind of tyranny whose priests are the advertising men. An attractive element in Buddhism for men of the materialistic West is what one might call its realism about sensual experience. An important part of the Buddhist practice of meditation is the relentless analysis of whatever has an appeal to the senses, and this harshly realistic attitude strikes one at first as providing a sharp and perhaps welcome contrast to the flattery and seduction of the senses which is so prominent a feature of modern materialism.

For instance, in the initial stages of Buddhist meditation a number of objects are recommended as being particularly suitable for aiding concentration and destroying mental and moral hindrances. Of the forty objects recommended in the great classic of Buddhist meditational practice, *The Way of Purification*, ten consist of corpses in various stages of decomposition. Meditation on any of these is said to be salutary for individuals in whom sensual desires are particularly strong: for example, 'the swollen corpse, as demonstrating the downfall of the shape of the body, is beneficial for one who lusts after beautiful shapes . . . the festering corpse, as demonstrating the bad stench which is bound up with the sores of the body, is beneficial for one who lusts after the odours of the body that are produced by flowers, perfumes and so on'; similarly for each of the ten.[1] Each one may be appropriate for a certain type of person. He must not turn away in squeamishness or horror, but contemplate the appropriate type of corpse steadily and long.

Not only the dead body is thus contemplated, however. Buddhist writings abound in passages which encourage one to regard the living human body as a disgusting accumulation of bones, skin, and filth, evil-smelling, always oozing and

[1] See E. Conze, *Buddhist Meditation* (1956), p. 104.

trickling from every aperture. 'It is a fundamental conviction for the majority of Buddhists', writes Edward Conze, 'that the body is an unclean thing, and that it is humiliating to have one. While we love it so much as we normally do, it should be seen for what it is, the passions it engenders must be burned out, the anxieties bound up with it must be overcome by being faced.' Meditational exercises which dwell on the disgusting aspects of the physical body are, he adds, 'useful to get us out of the fool's paradise in which we are wont to live'.

This is why, in Buddhist tradition, when a saintly monk is confronted with the sight of a dancing girl in a public place, one who has adorned herself in brave and alluring array, he is quick to analyse this meretricious glamour and to remember what a poor thing this collection of bones, fluid and skin really is, and to realise 'the misery of it all'.[1]

To the thoughtful person of any tradition there is nothing startlingly original in such ideas. But the fact that they are so prominent in Buddhism can be a mark in its favour in the eyes of one who is disillusioned with the contemporary world and its continual over-stimulation of the senses. To say anything more at this stage would be to anticipate discussion which must be left for later in the book, but it may be pointed out here that the appeal which Buddhism conceivably makes in this connection is due at least as much to the defective quality of contemporary Western culture as to the inherent strength of Buddhist thought.

Above all, however, the Buddha promises his followers a great peace, an end to restless desire and futile striving and worldly agitation. To the man of the twentieth century there may be something compelling about such a promise, especially when he sees it exemplified, in some degree at least, in the refinement of character and apparent tranquility of spirit of

[1] *Theragātha*, 300, 268 f., 463.

some public figure who is known to be a Buddhist. Such an impression has been made, for example, by U Thant, the Burmese Secretary-General of the United Nations. Here — in contrast to our noisy, restless world — one seems to encounter, however remotely, something of the profound peace which is expressed in the figure of the seated Buddha, deep in the contemplation of realities unknown to ordinary men.

FAITH WITHOUT RELIGION?

For reasons of this kind Buddhism has its special appeal for men of the twentieth century, and there are those who would hold that in some form or other it may be destined to be the world religion of the future; or rather, the *faith* of the future. For what is in some people's eyes a conclusive reason in favour of Buddhism is that it is not a 'religion' at all — that is, in the modern pejorative sense of the word.

It is claimed that Buddhism provides the perfect example of an essentially 'religionless' faith; it is our purpose here to show that this is not the case. Certainly Buddhism is formally agnostic. It is generally this aspect of Buddhism which is meant when people say that it is not a religion. Indeed, it has often been presented in Europe and America as simply a humanistic philosophy rather than a religious system. Not a few of those in western countries who regard themselves as followers of the Buddhist way of life would resist most vigorously the idea that Buddhism has from the beginning been bound up with an authoritative spiritual revelation, with a mythology, with a strictly disciplined religious life — in a word, with much of what is meant in the West by religion. It is with the fuller demonstration of this aspect of Buddhism that we shall soon be concerned. At this point we may note the attempts which are sometimes made by western writers to establish what they term 'original Buddhism', 'the Buddhism of the Buddha', or 'Buddhism as Gautama originally taught it'. The assumption behind such attempts is that what Buddhism has subsequently become in the lands of Asia to which it has now spread is only a sad corruption of its original pure nature as a humanistic philosophy.

But what Buddhism was in the sixth century B.C., no one can say with any certainty. Only the very rash, or the boldly speculative, or the incorrigibly fundamentalist, would claim to be able to separate 'original Buddhism' from what we now have in the Pali and Sanskrit texts. There is an interval of some four hundred years between the probable time of the Buddha's activity and the putting of pen to paper (or stylus to palm-leaf) to record what are now regarded as 'the words of the Buddha'. By that time Buddhism certainly appears as a religion, and it is only by speculation that one can sift out any so-called 'original philosophy', as some have claimed to be able to do. Such efforts inevitably entail the arbitrary rejection as 'late' and 'monkish' any evidence found in the texts which conflicts with the speculator's idea of what was original. There is nothing in the history of Buddhism which lends any firm support to the idea that we have here — or had at some point in the past — an example of a religionless faith. The Buddha may have criticized some of the religious aspects of the Brahmanism of his day, but it was out of a profoundly religious culture, i.e. that of ancient India, that Buddhism emerged; and, as soon as it had developed its own radical genius, it was as a religious movement that it appeared to the inhabitants of ancient India. That is to say it was a movement which was seen to be directly concerned with that which transcended mundane existence, and as such was explicitly opposed to the views and attitudes of the materialists and secularists of that day.

Meanwhile it will be the purpose of the next four chapters to convey something of the fundamentally religious quality of Buddhism as it exists today, and as it always existed, as far back in history as we can see. Few people would dispute the religious quality of Mahayana Buddhism. We shall therefore concern ourselves largely with the Theravada, as it is found in South-East Asia, the kind which is often regarded in the West as more a philosophy than a religion. It will be our purpose to show that to regard it so is to misunderstand it.

Part Two

BUDDHISM
AND
RELIGION

3

BUDDHISM AS A RELIGION

THE SOUTH-EAST ASIAN SETTING

O<small>N</small> a little hill just north of Burma's chief city, set in the wide green expanse of the Irrawaddy delta region, stands the great golden pagoda, the Shwe Dagon. Its tip is roughly the height above ground of the tip of the dome of St. Paul's Cathedral in London, and the sight of it in the brilliant sunshine invites the obvious and frequently used simile of a gigantic golden flame leaping up into the Burmese sky. Somewhere in the base of the central massive cone of the pagoda are said to be enshrined some hairs of the Buddha. This makes it a place of great sanctity to the Buddhist, and to this pagoda come the ordinary people of Burma in their thousands.

They may travel from distant mountain villages, perhaps on a pilgrimage for which they have waited and saved for many years. They may come from the city or the surrounding area, as they do on every Buddhist sabbath or holy day, to offer their homage to the Buddha, symbolized by the relics enshrined there. To them he is their great enlightener, and the stories of his life they know and love from their childhood. More than one Westerner, knowing the Buddhist people of Burma, has felt the impossibility of trying to convey the deep feeling which they have for the Buddha and his way of life, and the great peace to which he pointed them. At festival times they crowd the wide, smooth pavement that encircles the pagoda, they offer their homage, they recall the old legends, they chant quietly the precepts of their faith, and the slow deep boom of the gong speaks of merit acquired. Thus it is at many a pagoda throughout Burma — in Moulmein and Mandalay and Prome. The lay Buddhist lives simply, and has a moral code of five precepts: not to kill, not to steal, not to drink intoxicants, not to indulge in sexual misconduct, and not to speak untruths. On sabbath days he may add voluntarily a few more precepts, perhaps fasting all day. This is the religious framework of the lives of millions of lay Buddhists. In Asia, Buddhism is a religion.

But to know Buddhism one must know also the monasteries. In most Burmese towns there will be one or more. Inside the surrounding wall there will be a quiet, dusty garden, with a few ancient trees perhaps. The monastery itself consists usually of a number of huts, built of the hardwoods of the Burmese forest, and grouped round a central, larger hall in which the monks hold their assemblies and perform various occasional ceremonies. In his own small hut or cubicle the monk may engage for hours on end in the strenuous business of meditation. He sits on a mat, with legs crossed and back erect. He breathes regularly, silently counting each complete cycle of breathing, mentally watching the breath enter and leave his nostrils. His intention in doing this is to concentrate his mind to a single point, and to calm the restlessness of discursive thought, which leads nowhere — certainly not to salvation.

The background to this process of meditation, the sole basis upon which it can be undertaken, is a life of extreme simplicity by Western standards. The monks have a complicated code of morals, and their life in the community is governed by more

than two hundred rules, all of which must be carefully observed. A year or two ago, or perhaps ten or twenty, the monk's
head was shaved and he was presented with the orange-
coloured robe and the few small essential possessions that he is
allowed. After the ordination ceremony, conducted by the
abbot of the monastery to which he was seeking admission, he
entered the Order and has since then spent his time chiefly in
meditation, but possibly also in some study of Buddhist metaphysics, learning by heart long complicated lists of all the
various states of consciousness, their moral and psychic roots
(whether good, bad or neutral), and the multitude of their
possible combinations and future consequences.

He worships no God, at least as the word is usually understood in the West. To him the ultimate reality is the *Dharma*,
that which alone is self-subsistent. He venerates the Buddha as the
historical manifestation of the Dharma, but acknowledges that
Gautama, the Buddha for the present age, was fully human
and no divine phantom. By such continual meditation and
devotion the monk believes he will eventually attain to the state
of transcendental wisdom, the state of the extinction of all
passion, and therefore the end of all rebirth and redying — in a
word, nirvana. In the monasteries of Asia, also, Buddhism is a
religion.

THE REVEALED TRUTHS OF BUDDHISM

Like every historical religion, Buddhism is based on certain
truths which are acknowledged to have been perceived by one
whose superior insight and authority is recognized and accepted
without question by the adherents of this religion.

It is precisely this aspect of the matter which many modern
people in the West find difficult to accept, even when they
retain some kind of vestigial 'spiritual' belief: i.e. the idea of

accepting something on the spiritual authority of another person. Basically this refusal may be a form of self-conceit. In practice few people can be consistent in the refusal to accept any truth on the authority of another. We spend much of our lives thus accepting truths on other people's authority, and acting on them. Nevertheless, when it comes to spiritual matters, it frequently happens that people start to persuade themselves that they are independently-minded — rugged individualists who are not to be coerced into accepting anything they have not thought of themselves. This may sound an extreme way of putting it, but it is in effect what some people's prejudices in the realm of religious belief and practice often amount to. They do not wish their spiritual life to be bound by ancient creed, they say. They do not accept that there is any authority in 'sacred scripture'. Any suggestion of dogma (which they confuse with dogmatism) is quite abhorrent to them, and the idea of an authoritative revelation in spiritual matters is sheer obscurantism.

Is this a difficulty which western Christianity has unwarrantably put in people's way? Is it a peculiarity of the Christian Church? Shall we learn something of free thought from the East? Shall we perhaps find a more rational approach to things in Buddhism, for example? Those who think thus are due to be disappointed. The first affirmation which every Buddhist makes is this: 'I go for refuge to the Buddha.' That is to say, the first requirement is *faith* in the Buddha.

Here is what a leading Buddhist writer, Edward Conze, has to say on the subject: 'Bitter and incredible as it must seem to the contemporary mind, Buddhism bases itself first of all on the revelation of the Truth by an omniscient being, known as "the Buddha", and secondly on the spiritual intuition of saintly beings. In all disputes the ultimate appeal is, however, not to the "experience" of Tom, Dick and Harry, but to that of the fully-enlightened Buddha, as laid down in the "Buddha-word".[1]

Sthavira Sangharakshita makes the same point when he observes that the disciple does not take refuge in Gautama the Rationalist, or Gautama the Reformer, or even in Gautama the Arahat (that is, one who has achieved nirvana), but in Gautama the *Buddha*, the discoverer of the way to nirvana. The Buddha is distinguished from all those who, following in his way, have also become fully enlightened — that is, Arahats. 'We therefore honour the Master not only as an Arahat, or one by whom Nirvana has been attained, but as a Buddha who ... without a teacher and without a guide breaks through the obstacles which block the road to Nirvana.' This is pre-eminently the view found in the sacred texts, Sangharakshita observes. He goes on to say that 'the difference between a Buddha and an Arahat was not only clearly stated by the Master, but recognized and deeply felt by the disciples. Even when they had themselves attained to that freed state of consciousness which was the goal of the Teaching, they seem to have continued to feel that in some indefinable manner His realization immeasurably transcended their own'.[2]

The whole structure of Buddhist thought and practice thus depends on the authoritative word and example of the Buddha. The Buddhist way of life begins from the affirmation of faith, 'I go for refuge to the Buddha.' But besides the supreme authority of the Buddha himself, Buddhism recognizes the value of other spiritual authorities. As Edward Conze has written: 'Buddhism has much to say about the spiritual hierarchy of persons, for what someone can know and see depends on what he is. So the saint knows more than the ordinary person, and among the saints each higher grade more

[1] *Buddhist Thought in India* (1962), p. 30.
[2] *A Survey of Buddhism* (1959), pp. 43–45.

than the lower. In consequence, the opinions and experience of ordinary worldlings are of little account, on a level with the mutterings of housepainters laying down the law about Leonardo da Vinci's *Virgin on the Rocks*.'[1]

Other similar statements by Buddhists could be quoted, and reference could be made to the Buddhist scriptures, to show how fundamental to Buddhism is the idea of spiritual *authority* in matters relating to salvation. But enough has been said to make it clear that here is a way that is held to have been *revealed*, by one who was possessed of supernatural insight.

The total view of life set forth in Buddhism is regarded as being in essence that which the Buddha 'saw' when he became 'bodhi' — enlightened. It is this *true* view of the whole natural and supernatural world which is the content of the Buddha's frequently mentioned insight (*abhiññā*). What has thus been supernaturally perceived is the *Dharma*, and in this context the word Dharma means both 'revealed doctrine' and 'eternal truth'.

In essence, this may be set forth in a number of fairly concise propositions. For the benefit of those whose minds are not spiritually perceptive enough to grasp the truth which is thus presented to them in propositional form, however, there is the more elaborate exposition of the Dharma in the form of parables, stories and discourses. But in essence, all the vast body of didactic literature which goes to make up the central portion of Buddhist scripture known as the *Sutta-piṭaka* can be comprised in a few brief affirmations. The formula which Western readers may be most familiar with is that of the 'four holy truths'. The first of these is that all forms of existence whatsoever are subject to evil or ill (*dukkha*). But this way of stating the matter may be misleading for anyone who is not familiar with Buddhist thought. For, as Nyanatiloka points out, this does not refer

[1] *Buddhist Thought in India* (1962), p. 26.

simply to actual experience of the ills of life, but implies those
other two characteristic marks of all existence which in
Buddhist thought accompany the universality of evil. These
other two qualities are universal *impermanence (anicca)* and
absence of a permanent self (anatta) in anything or anyone. It is as a
consequence of this all-pervading law of complete impermanence that all phenomena, even the apparently most noble,
are subject to dissolution, and it is this that in Buddhist thought
renders them miserable, for they thus contain within themselves
the potentiality or germ of ill. This doctrine of the three universal
characteristics of existence is absolutely fundamental to
Buddhist belief. One cannot properly appreciate the force of the
Buddhist assertion that all existence is subject to ill (or
'suffering', as *dukkha* is sometimes translated) unless one understands in conjunction with this that everything is impermanent,
in a state of continual flux, and that nothing whatsoever abides
— nothing, that is, in the sense in which the worldling sees
things.

An important element in the Buddhist way of dealing
with this situation is a disciplined method of metaphysical
analysis aimed at disclosing this universal flux, and helping
men to recognize and realize it; and to realize it above all in
what they call 'themselves'. The Holy Eightfold Way, represented in the scriptures as revealed and proclaimed by the
Buddha, is the *way out* of this miserable state of affairs.

The first two terms in the eightfold way are right understanding and right thinking. To the one who is only at the
beginning of the Way, however, right understanding (that is,
of the true nature of things) is not yet possible. It belongs strictly
to the last stage of Buddhist progress, namely, the attainment of
transcendental wisdom. Only then can there be perfect perception
of the truth, in the sense in which the Buddha perceived it. At
the beginning, therefore, the understanding of existence which

the novice has, while it is a Buddhist understanding, is one which he owes to the perfect insight of the Buddha, who first revealed the (true) nature of things. This revelation of the truth has initially to be accepted in *faith*. Such trust in the revelation is the indispensable first step. A man may not at first fully understand that all existence is characterized by impermanence, nonentity and ill; at this stage he simply accepts the Buddha's word, taking the matter on trust.

The next three terms in the Buddhist way represent what follows on this initial attitude of faith, and are concerned with the moral life: right speech, right action and right livelihood. Together with faith, morality is the indispensable foundation of Buddhist life, for laymen and monks alike.

The three aspects of morality that are specifically emphasized here imply 'abstaining from lying, tale-bearing, harsh words and foolish babble' (*right speech*); 'abstaining from injuring living beings, from stealing, and from unlawful sexual intercourse' (*right action*); and rejecting a wrong means of livelihood, such as that of butcher or soldier, for one that is more in keeping with Buddhist sentiment (*right livelihood*).

Without this essential basis of a good moral life the practice of meditation which is outlined in the final three terms will be of no avail. But given this foundation, the essential and most characteristic feature of the Buddhist life can profitably be embarked upon. It is with this, namely meditation, that the final three terms, right (spiritual) effort, right mindfulness, and right concentration are concerned.

The term 'right effort' is one that assumes an acquaintance with the whole vastly complex and elaborate Buddhist system of analysis of mental states. Every conceivable state of mind is catalogued in a highly diversified analytical system, and each state is classified according to whether its dominant factors are evil or good or neutral. Having been versed in all this, the disciple has to strive to avoid the arising of evil states of mind, has to overcome evil states that have arisen, has to incite his will to encourage the arising of good states, and, once they have arisen, strive to preserve them and bring them to maturity. All this is meant by *right effort*.

Right mindfulness consists in contemplating the true nature of things, that is to say, not as they appear to the ordinary person who sees a being whom he identifies as John Brown, but as things really are and are seen by the well-practised Buddhist, who sees not John Brown but the impermanent flux of constituent physical and mental events which goes by the name of John Brown. More especially, it is for John Brown if he is a Buddhist to see 'himself' in this way.

Finally comes right concentration, when the disciple, detached from sensory objects and unwholesome states of mind, enters into a state of trance. When at last this has been achieved, as a result of faithfully accepting and following this path prescribed by the Buddha, then will ensue transcendental wisdom; and this consists of right understanding and right thinking. It was however from these two that the Buddhist disciple began: at the beginning, the understanding of things was one which he had to accept on trust, as an indispensable preliminary; now it is an understanding of things which he has by direct perception. The truth that was formerly known by faith only, is now known in itself as it is. But it is not the 'person' who is called 'John Brown' who knows this; the *bhavanga*, the stream of existence which was temporarily shaped as John Brown, this it is which thus enters into intimate awareness of the eternal truth.

Clearly we have in Buddhism a form of mysticism,[1] but it is a mysticism rooted in an attitude of faith — faith in the spiritual authority of the Buddha, of the Dharma he proclaimed, the

[1] On this see Trevor Ling, 'Buddhist Mysticism', in *Religious Studies* (Cambridge), vol. i, no. 2 (April 1966).

ideal of enlightened and purified man which he exemplified, and of the Sangha which also manifests and preserves and endorses this truth. Without this attitude of faith there would be no Buddhism. The Buddha's enlightenment and subsequent entry into nirvana is for the Buddhist the guarantee of the whole system. Buddhism might at first sight seem to be a kind of *lebensphilosophie*, a view of life which a man might eventually work out for himself simply by the penetrative power of his own thought. But the fact of nirvana is vouched for only by the Buddha. All runs back to this, and there is no reason for the Buddhist's confidence that such a state exists at all, apart from the Buddha. We are in fact confronted by what amounts to a claim to revelation.

Those who cannot accept that there is any reality which cannot be reached by man's unaided *intelligence* will find the idea of revelation no more acceptable simply because it is Buddhist revelation, rather than Christian, or Jewish, or Islamic. But at least some account should be taken of the fact that there is this type of revealed truth at the heart of a system of religious thought and practice which is wholly independent of the Hebrew and Christian tradition; and that the *abhiññā*, the 'supernatural insight' of the Buddha has provided the inspiration for the religious life of a large part of Asia.

4

BUDDHIST MYTHOLOGY

THE EXTENT OF BUDDHIST MYTHOLOGY

THE man of western upbringing who is attracted to
Buddhism because of what he believes to be its more
sophisticated approach to spiritual matters may be further
surprised at the extent of its mythology. 'I go for refuge to the
Buddha,' says the disciple, and, 'I go for refuge to the Dharma.'
We have already considered the Dharma, in essence, as it can
be set out in formal propositions. It is important to go on to
consider the very great elaboration which these essential truths
have received in practice. But first we must be clear about the
various meanings of the word Dharma.

The word is sometimes explained as though it meant simply
'the doctrine' or 'the law' by following which a man will come
at last to Enlightenment. This, it is true, is one of the senses in
which it is used. Its root, however, is in the verb *dhṛ* which
means to bear, or support, or uphold. Dharma is therefore the
great 'upholder' of all things, and in this sense it is translated as
'eternal truth', that which is absolute and underived.

It is important to notice that the Buddha is regarded not only
as the discoverer of eternal truth, but also as its *revealer*, or

discloser; that is to say, the one who himself *is* the manifestation of the Dharma. This is made quite explicit in Mahayana Buddhism, in what is known as the doctrine of the three 'Bodies' of the Buddha. This doctrine was actually formulated by a school of Buddhists known as the Yogacarins about A.D. 300, but there was nothing basically new in the substance of the doctrine. The idea that the historical Buddha, Gautama, was, in one aspect of his nature, to be identified with the Dharma is frequently found in the earlier history of Buddhism, and, as Conze points out, 'is of the essence of Buddhism.'[1] There is a saying of the Buddha recorded in the scriptures of the Theravada: 'He who sees the Dharma sees me; he who sees me sees the Dharma.'[2]

In the Buddhist view, until the Buddha reveals the eternal truth, i.e. the Dharma, it remains hidden and unknown. The Dharma has to be manifested historically. First, and above all, it has to be manifested in a human life; it has to be expressed in the form in which men can most easily and readily comprehend it. It is this historical manifestation of the eternal truth in a human life that Buddhists call the *nirmāna-kāya*, the 'conjured-up' body. So far as we in the present era of Buddhist history are concerned, the conjured-up body known to us is that of Gautama, the Buddha of the sixth century B.C. The next manifestation, the Buddha-who-is-to-come, will be Maitreya, according to the Buddhist texts. This idea of a fictitious, conjured-up or 'phantom' body which the eternal Dharma uses, so to speak, is likely to be regarded by Christians simply as an example of the Docetist heresy in a Buddhist context. But in fact, within the setting of Buddhism, this emphasis on the reality of the historical body has a quite different significance. It serves to emphasize that the *one* reality is the Dharma. Even

[1] *Short History of Buddhism* (1960), p. 36.
[2] *Samyutta-Nikāya*, iii. 120.

the Buddha, as he existed in Magadha in the sixth century B.C., real as he was, was only a transient phenomenon, existing solely in order to make known or convey to men the Dharma, which is supreme, eternal reality.

Thus the first sense in which the Dharma can be known by men is through an historical Buddha. Now the Buddha, the Buddha we know of, Gautama the man, is a congeries of events: of words spoken and deeds performed. We have to acknowledge that it is through these, initially at least, that the Dharma becomes known to men. Especially is this true of the words spoken. These constitute an important medium for the revealing of the Dharma. What the Buddha said, the whole collection of his sayings, is, therefore, also known as the Dharma. It is in this sense that the word Dharma is used to mean the doctrine, or the law.

In popular understanding the Dharma thus comes to connote the threefold collection of scripture, the Tripiṭaka. More especially, it comes to be identified with the second of the three collections, the Sutta Piṭaka. This is the section of the scriptures which is made up largely of stories of the Buddha and his early disciples, together with ancient Indian legends, and discourses based upon them. In this vast concourse of writings the Dharma is set forth in a great variety of ways. Sometimes it is in the form of a straightforward statement, which to those who are able to hear it contains a certain truth, that is to say it conveys the Dharma, and thus itself is — 'a dharma'. An example of this is to be found in that very popular collection of sayings known as the Dhammapada. First, a characteristically Buddhist statement is made: 'Never can hatred be appeased by hatred; it will be appeased only by non-hatred.' To this are then added the words: 'this is an everlasting dharma.'[1]

But the Dharma, the truth proclaimed by the Buddha in the

[1] *Dhammapada*, verse 5.

form in which we now have it in the Sutta-Piṭaka, is set forth
much more usually in stories of the Buddha, in legends, and old
myths refurbished for Buddhist purposes. Here essential
Buddhist truth is mixed, says Nyanatiloka, with 'conventional
truth' to 'suit the mind of the average man'.[1] Here are to be
found stories of sprites and ogres, gods and goddesses, demons
and monsters; here is ancient Indian legend and fable, stories of
miracles and visions of heavenly regions. For all this was
regarded by the men of ancient India as the scenery of the
natural world which surrounded them. In the more advanced
stages of Buddhist teaching a man is but a collocation of five
'khandhas' or separate constituent parts, but 'here [in the
Sutta-Piṭaka] men are called "men", trees "trees", and stones
are yet "stones". Slowly the *puthujjana*, the worldling, is
introduced to Truth, and the value of the higher life that alone
opens the path to deliverance'.[2] Thus the whole vast collection
of stories known as the Sutta-Piṭaka is the depository of the
Dharma. It is to this, in the first instance, that the Buddhist
goes 'for refuge'. Here he finds the Dharma in which he places
his faith. Here, within all this wealth of story and myth, is to
be found the Eternal Truth proclaimed by the Buddha, disclosed by the Buddha. That is the Buddhist contention. To ask
why it should be so — why truth should need to be diffused so
widely and presented in so many different forms — is to ask
why men's minds are what they are.

An objection may come from those who will say: admitted,
transcendent truth has to be mediated to men in forms that they
can comprehend; but the modern objection to mythology is
that this usually consists of religious truths expressed in terms
that are often not very far removed from animism, and in
categories that may be very different from the modern understanding of the world. This, of course, is undeniable. What is

[1] *Guide Through the Abhidhamma-Piṭaka* (1957), p. xiii.   [2] Ibid.

not admissible is the conclusion that is sometimes drawn from it, that in the modern age *all* forms of mythology are unnecessary and can be dispensed with.

The fact that Buddhism has been able to convey its truths to men in terms that are borrowed even from animism is really very remarkable, when we realize that animism represents an attitude to life which is the opposite of the attitude inculcated by Buddhism. As I have written elsewhere, the essence of the animistic attitude to life is that the ills which man experiences are attributed to wholly external forces. These forces, conceived as having an existence separate from his own, man regards as hostile. The essence of this attitude is that attention is focused on the *external* world. The desire of the individual to be re-released from insecurity or sickness, or to gain power or riches, or whatever other form his desire may take, is held to be realizable if the *external* world is dealt with in the right manner — by keeping out of the way of the demons that cause sickness or trouble, or preventing them from invading his body, or propitiating them, or invoking a stronger power.[1] In contrast to this is the attitude inculcated by Buddhism, which pays primary attention to the *inner* disposition of the man, and the deeper levels of the mind. It is evident that between these two attitudes to life there can be very little in common. In face of the evils of existence, popular naturalistic religion responds with action of an *external* kind; whereas a radical system of salvation such as Buddhism responds to these evils by the cultivation of a new *inner* attitude, by morality, by meditation and by seeking after transcendental wisdom. The mythology of Buddhism is the only common ground between what are in essence irreconcilable views of life.

[1] See the present writer's *Buddhism and the Mythology of Evil* (1962), p. 26.

THE FUNCTION OF BUDDHIST MYTHOLOGY

Why then has Buddhism allowed this open frontier between itself and animism? One part of the answer is that Buddhists have allowed this traffic between the Dharma and native animism *because Buddhism is a missionary religion*. It has been so from the beginning; the Dharma is something to be shared with all men, whoever they may be. If one desires to share the blessings of the Dharma with men who hold animistic ideas, then one must meet those men where they are, in their situation as animists. One must meet them there — but not leave them there. Rather, such people are to be encouraged and led towards a new and truer perspective, that of the Buddha and his teaching. To do this it is necessary first of all to use the kind of ideas and conceptions which they will be able to grasp, and with which they are familiar. This in fact is what historical Buddhism has done: it has, quite *spontaneously*, developed 'bridges' between popular ways of thought and the Dharma.

One such important bridge is the Buddhist symbol of Mara, the Evil One. This quite uniquely Buddhist mythological figure provides in practice a means of transition from animistic ideas to the profound analysis of existence that is involved in Buddhist meditation. At one end of his being the figure of Mara is akin to the demons of popular thought, the many evil spirits of Indian and South-East Asian folklore. He is a figure which the villager, coming into contact with Buddhist teaching for the first time, will recognize as something familiar. But there is a great deal in Buddhist teaching concerning Mara which goes beyond this popular and picturesque aspect of his nature. The new adherent of Buddhism would find in the teaching concerning Mara the idea of a power present everywhere in the world of the senses, a power hostile to the holy life, a power which resists the attempts of those who seek to follow the Buddhist way.

What is more, he would learn how complete was the Buddha's victory over this power, and he would learn of the victories over Mara gained by the early disciples who followed the Buddha on the path to Enlightenment. He would learn, in verse after verse of the scriptures, how he too might defeat Mara, and, being released from Mara's bonds and from his realm, might travel safely towards the Transcendent, towards nirvana. He would learn that the defeat of Mara depends on vigilant meditation, and the insight which follows. He would learn to see Mara, whom he had at first thought of as an evil spirit like those of his native folklore, no longer as a sort of village demon; rather he would see this enemy of the holy life through Buddhist eyes, as one of the early brethren was taught by the Buddha to see him. 'What is this Mara? Corporeality is Mara . . . feeling is Mara . . . perception is Mara . . . mental formations are Mara . . . consciousness is Mara.' In other words, Mara the evil one, the enemy, turns out to be much vaster, more sinister than the demon he appeared to be to the convert. He is seen to be co-extensive with the five constituents of human existence, the *khandhas*; he is the essence of this-worldly existence, that is to say, of all existence other than nirvana.

Thus the mythological symbol of Mara has been in actual practice a transitional concept, a bridge, a doctrinal *device* for leading men from the thought-forms of their native animism to the truth of the Dharma. Obviously there would have been those among the early Buddhists who would have 'seen through' this symbol of Mara, like the early disciple instructed by the Buddha, to whom we have just referred; these would have known that 'Mara' was but a symbol for realities which could be more succinctly expressed in the terms of the Buddhist metaphysics in which they themselves had now been instructed. They would have been fully capable of 'demythologizing'

Mara if they had wished to, and in some passages in the Buddhist scriptures, such as the one just quoted, this is in fact what is done. But if anyone had suggested that Mara should be permanently demythologized, that is expunged from Buddhist teaching, and his place taken by the abstract ideas which ultimately he represented, their reaction to such a proposal would probably have been, 'Why? Whatever for? What an absurd thing to want to do! How will the worldling, to whom we desire to preach the Dharma, be able to understand it without some familiar landmarks, like Mara?'

The Buddhist thus acknowledges the ways of attempting to understand the world that do exist among men, and says, in effect: 'If that is what you believe, and if that is how you see this life, let us start there!' And he proceeds to use this initial position as the taking-off ground for an approach to the eternal Dharma. Almost always he makes use of popular stories and legends. By far the most commonly known of Buddhist scriptures among the ordinary people are the Jātaka tales. These provide the principal religious diet for the ordinary Buddhist population of South-East Asia; they are known and loved and recited and acted and represented in colourful pictures in all the pagodas. They cannot be said to form anything more than a threshold to Buddhist belief; but it is a wide threshold and offers plenty of scope for all. Buddhism has in this matter, I believe, displayed considerable wisdom. But the important point to notice is that although Buddhism has thus allowed an open frontier between its own Dharma and animistic beliefs, this frontier has always been firmly controlled from the Buddhist side. What may be seen to have happened in the course of Buddhist history is not demythologizing, but a Buddhist-inspired *remythologizing* of popular thought: a recasting and refilling of potent psychological symbols as a result of the stimulus of Buddhist spiritual experience.

SOME LESSONS FOR DEMYTHOLOGIZERS

The religious role of mythology has been discussed here in Buddhist rather than Christian terms because in this way the subject can be viewed more objectively and with a sounder appreciation of the issues involved than when the matter is discussed in a purely Christian context. But from this discussion of the subject in its Buddhist setting certain conclusions seem to emerge which are of general interest.

It seems that, for the generality of men, *sacred truth has to be communicated in some form of story* if it is to be properly apprehended, and if it is to enter into the lives of ordinary people in such a way as to affect the springs of feeling and volition. If anyone should object that this is unnecessary in the case of modern, sophisticated men of the twentieth century, I would point in reply to the methods used in advertising today, particularly in commercial television. Let the reader test this for himself, and notice how almost any idea has to be communicated to the public through the medium of a 'story', even if this is only the portrayal of some very familiar domestic situation. This analogy is however to some extent misleading. The stories through which sacred truths are realized are not manufactured specially for the purpose. They are at hand, ready made, in the mythological material that is for ever being thrown up from the human unconscious.

Modern secularism may seem just as irreconcilable as animism is to the essential truths of Buddhism, and, one might equally well say, to the essential truths of Christianity. From the Buddhist and the Christian point of view there is not a lot to choose between animism and modern secularism; between the man whose vision is limited to the confines of the primeval jungle, and the man whose vision is limited to the confines of the concrete jungle. What the modern 'plain man' is really objecting to, when he says that he cannot stomach the mythological element in Christianity, is not the fact that there is *a* mythology, but that it is not *his* mythology, or that it does not seem to be relevant to his understanding of the world, moulded as it is as much by unconscious as by conscious assumptions.

It is to this aspect of the matter that Rudolph Bultmann's well-known proposals for demythologizing the Christian gospel fail to do justice. As many of his critics have pointed out, Bultmann, in his concern to make the gospel relevant to the man of the twentieth century, tends to overlook the fact that the common man, even in the twentieth century, is not commonly an existentialist philosopher. Men do, in fact, possess an ineradicable tendency to myth making. The theory of C. G. Jung, that mythology is the perennial product of the collective or universal unconscious in which all men share, has been seen by many to throw much light on ancient mythology and modern psychological case-histories. As Helmut Thielicke writes, in connection with the mythological element in the New Testament, this is due 'not to historical circumstances, or to the contemporary world-view, but to the way man looks at things. We can no more abandon mythology than we can cease to think in terms of time and space'.[1] Not demythologizing, but *remythologizing*, would seem to be our real need today; the recovering and reinstating of powerful images and thought-symbols which provide men with a common ground between the everyday and the eternal, instead of the unredeemed secular mythologies with which so much of modern life is impregnated, and which are, more often than not, only a common ground between earth and hell.

[1] 'The Restatement of New Testament Mythology', in *Kerygma and Myth*, ed. H. W. Bartsch (London, 1960), p. 141.

5

THE SOCIAL DIMENSION
OF BUDDHISM

THE SANGHA AND THE SPREAD OF BUDDHISM

THERE is a remarkable catholicity about Buddhism, a feature which it shares with Islam and Christianity. The writer's own first contact with Buddhism was in the hills of North Bengal, in the course of war service. There, one was not far from Tibet, and the little Buddhist states of Bhutan and Sikkim. In Gangtok, the capital town of Sikkim, a chance encounter and an almost night-long conversation with an English officer who had come down from Tibet, where he and a small detachment were stationed, afforded a near glimpse of the Buddhism of that country. What seemed fascinating was the fact that an Indian religion could take so strong a hold upon the formerly warlike tribes who lived on the high Tibetan plateaux among snow and ice and tempest, and could inspire them with its tenets of gentleness and benevolence, and enable them to produce so elaborate and magnificent a system of ritual, and disciplined meditation. This is a remarkable achievement, and one of the outstanding examples of Buddhist missionary expansion.

In Ceylon one finds another example of Buddhism's ability

to take root outside the land of its origin, this time in a region as different from Tibet as can possibly be imagined: a rich, fertile tropical island, a place of lush vegetation and languid climate. In the vibrant heat of Ceylon life is profuse and luxuriant, and one might suppose, cheap. But not so. The Buddhist reverence for life has imposed itself on the earlier culture of the island, and to many of the people of Ceylon even the swatting of a mosquito would be a demeritorious act. And here, in spite of the recent entanglement of some of the monks in politics, for most of them the proper concern of the monk is what it has always been, to engage in meditation — day after day, year after year, and thus to climb those upper stretches of the path to nirvana which every Buddhist hopes he may one day tread, in some future existence if not in this present one. The meditation which is practised in the monasteries of Ceylon beneath the tropical sunshine is basically the same as that which is practised among the snows of Tibet.

From Ceylon to Burma and Thailand is not a great distance geographically, but it is culturally. One has left behind the Sanskrit civilization and language of India and Ceylon, and now it is of the proximity of China that one is chiefly aware. Here, too, one finds how completely the people have made this Indian religion of the Buddha their own. And not only here; even in Burma and Thailand Chinese pagodas and monasteries are to be found, reminders of the fact that the religion of the Buddha has for many centuries been accepted by large numbers of the Chinese race. One recalls how from that country it spread to Korea, and thence to Japan, and there took root among the vigorous, industrious Japanese; and how, finally, in modern times it has travelled from Ceylon and Japan to Europe and America.

In this story of Buddhist expansion one is reminded of the remarkable capacity which Buddhism possesses for gathering within the community of those who follow the way of the Buddha men and women of diverse religions and races. It is important to remember that at the heart of Buddhism there is a community, the Sangha, the order of monks, which is one and the same throughout the Buddhist world (apart, that is, from slight differences of emphasis and usage). It is this, more than any other single factor, which explains the spread of Buddhism throughout the world and its survival throughout the centuries.

This is important, because many people in the West today, while they may agree about the desirability of some kind of ethical or religious belief, are entirely sceptical about the necessity or even the value of religious institutions, of which the Buddhist Sangha is an example: a community to which men and women commit themselves, sharing its traditions, receiving its benefits, accepting the various demands which it makes upon them.

BUDDHISM AND COMMUNITY

It is worth noting that among some of the earliest Buddhists there appears to have been a distrust of any kind of human association, even for religious purposes. In the *Sutta Nipāta*, one of the oldest sections of Buddhist literature, there is a poem entitled 'The Rhinoceros', which warns the man who would seek enlightenment against the fetters of family life and even ordinary friendship; he is urged to forsake the pleasures of society of every kind, and instead to withdraw into absolute isolation and solitude.

Some of the earliest Buddhists do seem in fact to have led just such a hermit-like existence. This emerges from those songs which tell of the spiritual struggles of the saints of the early days.[1] The insistence upon absolute solitude which is found in these

[1] *Psalms of the Brethren* (Theragāthā), and *Psalms of the Sisters* (Therīgāthā).

poems is not surprising, for the follower of the Buddha, in his total rejection of the world of sensory existence, would, initially at least, have been inclined to turn his back on the rest of the human world, as something that dangerously fettered him to that from which he was seeking to escape. The Theravada Buddhist ideal is the Arahat (what in modern terms we might call the 'go-it-alone saint'), and Professor T. R. V. Murti, from the point of view of Mahayana Buddhism, has pointed out what *in theory* this Theravada ideal seems to imply: 'the Arahat rests satisfied with achieving his own private salvation; he is not necessarily and actively interested in the welfare of others. The ideal of the Arahat smacks of selfishness; there is even a lurking fear that the world would take hold of him if he tarried here too long.'[1]

From a theoretical point of view this statement is irrefutable, and one is inclined to wonder how there came to be a *Sangha*, a Buddhist community of monks at all. As S. Dutt has pointed out, 'in numerous passages of Buddhist canonical literature settled life in a monastery is not contemplated at all, and the ideal for a bhikkhu is set out to be a free, unsocial, eremitical one.'[2] The fact remains, however, that this kind of solitary life later became largely an ideal, and actual practice among the Buddhist ascetics of ancient India diverged more and more from it — although not without some sense of conflict between the two different ways of life.[3]

It must be remembered, of course, that the eremitical ideal was well known in ancient India. The homeless religious ascetic was a common feature of Indian life at the time of the Buddha, and is by no means peculiar to early Buddhism. There were, apparently, mendicants of all kinds, holding various religious views and doctrines. In fact, what distinguishes

[1] *The Central Philosophy of Buddhism*, p. 263.
[2] *Early Buddhist Monachism* (1924), p. 112.   [3] Ibid., pp. 117 f.

Buddhism from other contemporary sects (most of which have long since disappeared) is the eventual establishment among Buddhists of the monastic life. The actual occasion for this, probably, was provided by the common practice of retiring to a sheltered retreat for the rainy season, together with other wandering ascetics. In origin this custom was presumably nothing more than an enforced necessity during the season of the tropical rains in India, when travelling about the land would have been a physical impossibility. In this matter Buddhist ascetics merely followed the practice that was common among all such mendicants. In their case, however, this institution of the rains retreat developed into something else; it became the forerunner out of which came the setting up of permanent colonies, or *avasas*. In this respect the Buddhist practice was not common to all. Others did not follow their example; the rains retreat remained in their case a purely temporary gathering of chance acquaintances — if 'acquaintances' is not too strong a term for those who merely shared a common physical proximity.

Why then did a community life develop in the case of the followers of the Buddha? What was it that gave the additional impulse in their case, whereby the rains retreat developed into a permanent form of settled corporate life?

The impulse may have come from the characteristic emphasis on following the middle path between extremes, which lies very close to the heart of Buddhist practice. In this case the middle path would consist of an avoidance of the snares of worldly life on the one hand, and of the extreme rigours of eremitical existence on the other. Bishop Bigandet, from his own observation of Buddhism in Burma in the middle of the nineteenth century, noted that although the principle of renunciation, which was still practised by Brahman anchorites, was cherished and admired by Buddhist bhikkhus also, nevertheless 'the mode of carrying it into practice is more mild and more consonant with reason and modesty'.[1] The practice of the middle way may thus provide a large part of the answer for the change to monastic life, but this may not be the whole answer. It is possible that an unconscious awareness of the need for a community wherein the Dharma could be preserved and taught and practised was also making itself felt. Whatever the reason may be, the bhikkhus developed a corporate life.

Nevertheless, because the eremitical tradition is so strong in Indian religion, earlier practice persisted, side by side with the more moderate form of withdrawal from the world into the life of the monastery. Until the latter finally prevailed in Buddhism there remained for some time those who preferred the older form of the religious life. That is to say, in the period reflected by the canonical scriptures, the characteristic Buddhist spirit of the avoidance of extremes in matters of religious practice had not yet fully worked itself out in the life of the Sangha; the situation was somewhat similar to that of the early Christian Church during its first few years, when it still lived the life of a sect within Judaism, and old customs were still observed by force of habit.

THE COMMUNITY'S CENTRAL CONCERN

In thus becoming corporate in form, Buddhism did not, however, lose anything of its essentially contemplative nature. It was in the life of the monastic community that the disciplines and exercises of meditation were developed and transmitted. And in promoting and developing the practice of meditation, as far as Theravāda Buddhism is concerned, the Sangha in Burma has played a prominent part. From Burma new

[1] *The Life, or Legend of Gaudama, the Buddha of the Burmese* (Rangoon, 1866), p. 487.

developments in the practice of meditation have spread to other Theravāda countries. Bhikshu Sangharakshita, in his *Survey of Buddhism*, notes that during the last fifty years the practice of respiration-mindfulness has undergone a remarkable revival in Burma, and that 'the contemporary heirs of the Arahats of old are supplementing scriptural knowledge by personal experimentation and experience'.[1] It is noteworthy too that Nyanaponika Thera of Ceylon has given to his book in which he describes the 'new Burman Satipatthāna Method' of meditation the title: *The Heart of Buddhist Meditation*. In this he describes the method which he learnt from a meditation master in Burma, where, he adds, 'the earnest practice of Satipatthāna is widely spread and is steadily progressing'.[2]

Enough has been said to indicate that the pursuit of the contemplative life has been, and still is, the central concern of a highly influential section of the Buddhist Sangha in Burma. The significance of this fact, in connection with the Sangha's social influence, will now be seen as we turn to consider the relation of the monasteries to the life of the people.

THE COMMUNITY AND SECULAR SOCIETY

The Buddha–Dharma has no direct and immediate bearing on the social organization of secular life; like Christianity, Buddhism is not committed to any one particular doctrine of society. The statement of the Buddha concerning the Vajjians,[3] a federation of republican tribes, that so long as they assembled regularly and in good numbers they might expect to prosper, is probably best understood as a simple statement of fact, and not as implying direct Buddhist approval of a republican system. As a modern exponent of Buddhism puts it:

[1] Op. cit., p. 158.
[2] Op. cit. (Colombo, 1956), p. 5.   [3] *Dīgha Nikāya*, ii. 73.

'Buddhism has no objection to a socialistic or to a capitalistic state provided it makes provision not only for the material but also for the moral and spiritual well-being of its subjects'.[1]

This does not mean, however, that the life of a people is likely to be uninfluenced by the existence within it of a community whose chief aim it is to live the contemplative life. The reproach levelled against the Theravādins by the Mahāyānists has already been noted, regarding what appears to be the essentially selfish character of the Arahat ideal, and the consequent neglect of the rest of men and their welfare. In this, as in many other matters regarding the relation of the Theravādins to the Mahāyāna, it is necessary to see things in proper perspective. The doctrines that are held must be examined in relation to their effect in practice, and not merely in theoretical isolation. And in practice the Theravāda Sangha has a record of social influence which, in Burma at least, where the radical Abhidhamma tradition of the monasteries has been strong from the earliest period,[2] has been remarked upon by a number of observers, whether they were wholly sympathetic towards Buddhism or not.

Bishop Bigandet, the nineteenth-century Roman Catholic bishop of Ramatha, a careful student of Burmese Buddhism, and one by no means given to lenient judgements of it, described the Sangha of his day at considerable length, and had a good deal to say about its influence on the life of the country. 'When we speak of the great influence possessed by the religious Order of Buddhist monks, we do not intend to speak of political influence,' he writes. 'It does not appear that in Burma they have ever aimed at any share in the management or

---

[1] B. Sangharakshita in *2500 Years of Buddhism*, ed. P. V. Bapat (Delhi, 1956), p. 449. For the view that Buddhism in South-East Asia has tended to be more receptive to a socialist rather than a capitalist form of society see below, Chs. 7 and 8.

[2] See N. R. Ray, *Theravada Buddhism in Burma* (Calcutta, 1946), p. 259.

direction of the affairs of the country. . . .[1] But in a religious point of view alone, their influence is a mighty one. Upon that very Order hinges the whole fabric of Buddhism. From it, as from a source, flows the life that maintains and invigorates religious belief in the masses that profess that creed. We may view the members of the Order as religious, and as instructors of the people at large, and principally of youth. In that double capacity, they exercise a great control and retain a strong hold over the mind of the people.'[2]

This short quotation is fairly representative of the whole chapter which Bigandet devotes to the subject. While he does not fail to speak of abuses which have crept into the Sangha, he is, he says, desirous of dealing with the life of the Sangha fairly and impartially, for this it well deserves. Others echo the same sentiments. 'In Burma, Buddhism has penetrated more deeply than in Ceylon into the life of the people', wrote H. Hackmann, 'and has given it more of its colour. Perhaps it is here that the religion of Gautama won its most real and attractive present-ment. . . .'[3] Sir J. G. Scott[4] and H. Fielding Hall,[5] each an authority on Burmese life, pay similar tributes to the respect paid to the Sangha by the people of Burma, and the influence it exerts in the common life. Nihar Ranjan Ray, in his history of Theravāda Buddhism in Burma, writes: 'It would be a sad mistake to suppose that the Buddhist monks of Burma live an isolated and self-complacent existence. Indeed, nothing could be further from the truth. . . . In fact the Sangha constituted an

[1] This is no longer true. For the recent participation of monks in political movements in Burma see the article by Cecil Hobbs in *Far Eastern Economic Review*, xxi (1956), pp. 586-99.

[2] Bigandet, *The Life, or Legend of Gaudama, the Buddha of the Burmese* pp. 523 f.

[3] *Buddhism as a Religion* (London, 1910), p. 126.

[4] *The Burman* (London, 1882), vol. i, ch. iv, especially pp. 44 f.

[5] *The Soul of a People* (London, 1904), pp. 123-39.

essential element — by far the most effective and powerful element — of the entire social fabric of the peoples of Burma.'[1] The Sangha, he says, has given to Burma a society based on equality of social standards, without distinction of wealth or caste, and very few countries in Asia enjoy such a democratic social life as Burma does. 'No doubt the high ethical and spiritual values of Buddhism and the generally high moral tone of the Sangha were the main inspiration that drew people to the services of the monks and their organization; but one cannot but recognize that the people were deeply conscious of the services rendered to them by the monks.'[2]

So far we have seen that the central concern of the most influential members of the Sangha in Burma is with the practice of meditation, and that it is this which earns for the Sangha the profound veneration of the people, and enables its influence to have a high ethical and spiritual value. But besides this, another factor has to be taken into account, and that is the accessibility of the monasteries. Between the monks and the people there is a constant communication and discourse. The monk, writes Fielding Hall, 'is not cut off from society . . . there are visitors, men and women. He may talk to them — he is no recluse; but he must not talk too much about worldly matters.'[3] This accessibility of the monks is the feature which J. B. Pratt fastened on as distinguishing the Burmese Sangha from that of Ceylon. Comparing the Buddhism of these two countries he comments: 'One gets the impression that it fills a much larger place in the life of the Burmese laymen than in that of the Ceylonese. The monasteries of Ceylon are frequently in very remote regions, appropriate for the solitary meditation of the three or four monks who dwell in them, but difficult of access from the town or village; whereas in Burma they are much more likely to be found near the centres of population,

[1] Op. cit., p. 266.   [2] Ibid., pp. 266 f.   [3] Op. cit., p. 123.

56

The Social Dimension of Buddhism

and are in fact located there purposely so that the laymen may come thither for their devotions and the little boys for their studies.'[1] The fact that, until recently, the majority of Burmans received at least some of their schooling in the monasteries, which were also the village schools, indicates another of the close links between the life of the monastery and the life of the people.

The special characteristics of the Buddhist Sangha at its best are thus seen to be: first, the constant cultivation of those insights concerning human existence which are to be found in the Abhidhamma; and second, complete accessibility to the people. Both are equally important; social contact and inter-course are essential if the ethical and spiritual values of Buddhism are to be transmitted to the surrounding society; equally essential is the faithful practice of the contemplative life, if what is transmitted is to be worth transmitting and is to have an ennobling effect. It is with regard to the first of these that radical forms of religion elsewhere have sometimes failed; they have lost touch with the society around them; thus the word 'pietism' becomes synonymous with social irresponsibility, or ineffectiveness.

We have already noted, in connection with Buddhist mythology, the way Buddhism has allowed an open frontier between radical religious insight and popular belief. The fundamental incompatibility between the Buddha-Dharma and animistic ways of thought and practice is, of course, fully accepted by the more learned Buddhist monks.[2] Nevertheless it is the Sangha that has allowed, and indeed has been respon-sible for establishing, a common ground between Buddhism and animism. 'The Buddhist monks thus played the most important social role of civilizing a primitive mind through a

---

[1] *The Pilgrimage of Buddhism* (London, 1928), p. 126.
[2] See Ray, op. cit., pp. 268 f., and Hackmann, op. cit., p. 150.

process of rational synthetization and yet without letting it feel
that it was being cut off from its tribal and primitive moorings.'[1]
The fact that these monks themselves are not cut off from their
own radical Buddhist moorings must, it seems, be due to the
existence among them of at least a nucleus of men who are
deeply engaged in the profounder experiences of meditation;
and who are also sharply aware of the ultimate incompatibility
of outlook between animism and Buddhism, and the need for
vigilance. If there were not such guardians of the radical element
in the background the Buddhist monks could have no
civilizing role to play: the Sangha would soon become indistinguishable from those whom it should be benefiting. The
fact that in Burma the study of the Abhidhamma and the kind
of meditation associated with it have been so widely pursued
may help to explain the relatively healthy condition of
Theravāda in that country. Those whose constant occupation is
with these matters will inevitably communicate much of the
essential bearing and spirit of Buddhism to those fellow-
members of their community who are more closely involved in
the popular religion. The indispensable element in this situation
is *the community* itself, where the spirit of the higher religion can
have free course among the members and preserve the essential
insights of the Buddhist faith. Eliot gives his judgement that it
is chiefly to the existence of the community, the Sangha, that
the permanence of the Buddha's religion is due.[2]

In conclusion, therefore, it may be said that the Buddhist
Sangha illustrates this: that a radical, contemplative form of
religion, *even when it is most faithful to its own characteristic
emphases*, is not necessarily insular or individualistic in form, or
socially ineffective. But if it is to endure amid surrounding
popular beliefs with which it is not in harmony, it must be
embodied in a community within which its own special insights

[1] Ray, op. cit., p. 269.   [2] *Hinduism and Buddhism*, i. 237.

are the accepted criteria of thought and action. In the continuing life of this community those insights will be preserved and transmitted to the society within which it exists. But if the community is to continue to exert a beneficent influence on the life of the people, the members of the community must have as their *primary* concern the maintaining, fresh and inviolate, of these special insights which are the essence of their faith.

6

BUExhDDHIST DEVOTION

THE EMPHASIS ON PRACTICE

RELIGIOUS statements, such as those which Buddhism provides in abundance, may be examined critically by the linguistic philosopher, and he may or may not judge them to have intelligible meaning. But Buddhists would hold that this kind of procedure is in itself incomplete and misleading. It is a strange fact that the welter of words in Buddhism is a testimony to the ultimate inadequacy of words. The apparently never-ending flow of discourse and exhortation, precept and illustration, story and legend which make up the Buddhist scriptures arises in large measure out of the recognition that words by themselves have only a limited capacity to convey religious truth and stir and maintain religious faith.

Only a man who is extremely well-attuned spiritually, it is said, will grasp the principle of the non-existence of the 'self' when it is expressed in its barest form in the idea that the self does not reside in the five *Khandhas*, i.e. the five basic physical and mental factors which produce the illusion of a 'self'. One who is somewhat less perceptive may discern this truth on the basis of a slightly fuller analysis and exposition — in terms of the twelve *āyatanas*;[1] the less perceptive still on the yet fuller basis of the eighteen *dhātus*.[2] But for most men the exposition of the doctrine in these abstract terms will in any case need to be followed up, elaborated and illustrated in terms of Buddhist story and legend before it begins to be apprehended in any genuine sense. And even such elaboration is not finally enough, if it remains purely intellectual. For Buddhism as a religious system implies that verbal statements alone cannot enable a man to grasp transcendental truth. It is recognized in Buddhism that such statements, divorced from other media of perception, may be misleading or harmful. Buddhists never tire of emphasizing that if one wishes to understand Buddhism one must practise it. There are other ways of approaching reality apart from that of logical statement. These other media correspond very closely to what in Christian terminology are known as sacramentals, and they are very important in Buddhism. An exponent of the Buddhist way has in fact called it 'truth . . . poured into the mould of religious observance'.[3]

It is this aspect of the study of Buddhism which has in the past often been neglected by Western students. Yet in its beginnings in ancient India Buddhism was essentially a matter of 'the holy life', and as it exists today in Asia this is still its essential feature. The living of the holy life is something common to both monks and laymen. The practical details will vary considerably; for the monk there will be regular daily devotion and the observance of moral precepts, and to this will

[1] These are the twelve 'bases' of mental processes; they consist of (*a*) the organs of the six senses (sight, hearing, smell, taste, touch, and, included by Buddhists, thought) together with (*b*) their corresponding objects, visible, audible, etc.

[2] These consist of the twelve *āyatanas* with the addition of the six kinds of consciousness which arise in connection with each of the six senses, i.e. consciousness of seeing, consciousness of hearing, etc.

[3] P. Dahlke, *Buddhist Essays*, pp. 337 f.

be added periods of active meditation. For the layman devotion and moral living will be his concern largely, although he too may sometimes engage in the practice of meditation.

That Buddhist devotional practice is often overlooked by Western students of religion may perhaps be due to a misunderstanding of the Buddha's well-known refusal to acquiesce in the sacrificial practices of Brahmanism. Certainly a good deal is said in early Buddhist literature that is critical of the rites of the Brahmans.[1] But it would be wrong to conclude from this that Buddhism in practice is, or has ever been, opposed to the use of sacramentals. Indeed, it is a notable feature of Buddhism that spiritual doctrine and ritual practices are held together in a harmonious relationship.

This is particularly important in view of the condition of Western religion today, where such a harmony of these two elements is less common. If a man is a Christian he has no choice but to belong to one of the two main varieties of Christianity, Catholic and Protestant. It is an invidious choice to have to make, since each variety is open to well-grounded objections from the other. Catholicism offers a rich *sacramental* life; it recognizes that mortal and finite man must use symbols, rites and sacramental disciplines of various kinds to make more real the spiritual dimension, and to help pierce the veil between the human world and that which is eternal and holy. But Catholicism is frequently characterized also by theological dogmatism, by the assumption that religious truth is capable of being contained in propositional form, in systematic or dogmatic theology; and that men must assent to these propositions or be classed as heretics, and unworthy of the benefits of religion.

By contrast Protestantism, while in many of its varieties it rejects the dogmatism of the Catholic Church, and affirms liberty of conscience and understanding where religious matters

[1] See, for example, the Kūṭadanta Sutta of the *Dīgha Nikāya*.

62

are concerned, is nevertheless lamentably weak as far as sacramental and ritual practice is concerned. There is, as a leading Protestant writer, Paul Tillich, has pointed out, no genuine sacramental basis in Protestantism; it has become a highly intellectualized affair, drained of all numinous quality; religious reality is dissolved in rationalism and moralism.[1]

Buddhism, on the other hand, is much more generally and widely characterized by a well-established harmony between a tolerant faith and an unselfconscious ritual. This has long been recognized as true of Japanese Buddhism, for example, in its classic forms. One of the features of Shingon commented upon by Sir Charles Eliot is the alliance of an unauthoritarian yet persuasive view of life with a deep-reaching mystic ritual.[2] So far as Theravada Buddhism is concerned, however, this might be thought to be less likely to provide so good an example of a balanced religious system, especially if one were to rely on the accounts of the Theravada provided by some European writers. In general, there has been a tendency in the West to overemphasize the differences between the Theravada and other schools of Buddhism — as though there were here something of the same kind of division as that which exists between Catholic and Protestant Christianity. This is an unjustifiable view of the Theravada, which in its essential features is much closer to the Buddhism of China and Japan than Protestant Christianity is to Catholic.

The reason for this mistaken view of Theravada is probably to be found in the fact that it was through the Pali scriptures that the Theravada first became known to the West, and in the religious atmosphere of nineteenth-century Europe it was thought sufficient to judge a religion by the scriptures it had produced. The actual religious life of Buddhist Burma or

[1] See P. Tillich, *The Protestant Era* (London, 1951), pp. 228 f.
[2] *Japanese Buddhism*, p. 340.

Thailand has therefore remained to a much greater extent unknown. This is why the occasional visitor from the West who thinks he knows Theravada from its scriptures, or the books based on them, is surprised when he comes in contact with it as it is in South-East Asia. 'But surely,' he says (as the writer has heard people say at the Shwe Dagon pagoda in Rangoon, as they observed Theravada shrines, rites, and devotions), 'surely, this is Mahayana!'

Such an observer soon finds that he must adjust his view of Theravada Buddhism. He learns that it makes much of sacred places; sacred because of their historical associations, or because of some relic of the Buddha which they enshrine, or of some Buddhist saint. He becomes aware of the deep reverence with which, in Burma, the Buddhist layman or monk regards these sacred places, and of the obviously deep devotion which is offered there.

DEVOTIONAL PRACTICE AT THE PAGODA

There are, as we have seen already, two focal points in the Buddhism of South-East Asia: the pagoda, and the monastery; often they will be found in close proximity.

The pagoda is a manifestation of lay devotion to the Buddha. Originally, in ancient India, it was a mound in which were enshrined sacred relics. Nowadays its shape has become somewhat altered, so that the semi-spherical solid base is elongated upward, tapering gracefully to a thin neck, and widening again to a finial, surmounted very often by a metal parasol, to which tiny bells may be attached, and which, stirred by the breeze, make a continual gentle music. Within the solid base of the pagoda is a sealed chamber usually containing some object of special sanctity or importance — ashes of a Buddhist saint, an ancient text, or some other holy relic. This massive structure, either of stone or of brick and plaster, is usually whitewashed, or, in the case of the larger pagodas in such cities as Bangkok, Rangoon and Mandalay, covered with pure gold leaf. The pagoda proper is often surrounded by small personal or family shrines containing *Buddha-rupas* (usually known in Western parlance as Buddha-images). At these shrines the lay people of the neighbourhood will offer their devotions, facing towards the central mass of the pagoda, which symbolizes for them their Lord, the Buddha, the revealer of the way to enlightenment and peace.

The outward form of such devotion usually takes the form of the offering of flowers, lights and incense. The flowers are placed before the image of the Buddha to the accompaniment of a set form of words, in Pali, such as the following:

These flowers, fresh-hued, sweet-scented and choice,
I offer at the sacred, lotus-like feet of the Noble Sage.

With many flowers the Buddha I adore,
And through this merit may there be release.

Even as these flowers must fade,
So does my body march to destruction.

Simple earthenware lamps containing coconut oil or camphor are then lighted (or, in Burma and Thailand, more usually candles), and are placed by the worshipper at the edge of the shrine, again to the accompaniment of a Pali verse:

With lamps brightly shining, abolishing the gloom,
I adore the Enlightened One
That light of the three worlds, who dispels the darkness
(of ignorance).

Similarly again with the offering of incense, an appropriate verse is chanted. 'By making such material and mental offerings', writes a modern Buddhist, 'the devotee expresses, and thus strengthens, his attitude of devotion towards the Buddha.'[1] The Ven. H. Saddhatissa Thera of Ceylon, in the preface to his collection of *Suttas* or verses used in Buddhist worship, writes of the 'great necessity in the religious life of the average man and woman' of the performance of such actions, and emphasises the *psychological* effect that is produced by the recitation of these suttas.[2] In conversation with the present writer he expressed his concern that in the West some adherents of Buddhism should consider such regular devotion unnecessary.

At the pagoda various suttas of this kind may be quietly recited by the devotee, including salutation of the holy relic, desire for forgiveness of faults, homage to the Buddha, the Dharma and the Sangha, and a request to share with all beings any merit acquired. This last intention is also indicated by the striking of a deep-toned gong; this the worshipper does upon leaving the shrine, and as the sound reverberates, so he would have his merit spread out and shared. Sometimes lay people will use their visit to the pagoda as an opportunity for meditation also, using perhaps one of the traditional subjects, as may be appropriate — the impure nature of the physical body, or death, or the Buddha, or love.

DEVOTIONAL PRACTICE AT THE MONASTERY

The other focal point of Buddhist devotional practice is the monastery. Primarily the place of residence for the monks, the lay people resort there on special occasions to join with the

[1] Bhikshu Sangharakshita, *Survey of Buddhism* (Bangalore, 1959), p. 448.
[2] *Handbook of Buddhists* (Banaras, 1956), pp. i f.

monks in their devotions. There is a daily office which the monks say together, morning and evening.[1] It is on the fortnightly *Uposattha* day, loosely called the Buddhist sabbath, that the people of the village or the surrounding area will attend one or other of these services. They are sometimes invited to attend by the sounding of a bell or a drum. The service takes place in a large assembly hall, before a Buddha image. The people bring their offerings of flowers, lights and incense, as at the pagoda, and present them before the devotions begin. After the offerings have been made and the candles lit, the whole assembly bows to the image of the Buddha. Obeisance is a common element of Buddhist practice, both religious and social. Full obeisance, in the course of religious devotion, consists in touching the ground with knees, forehead and elbow. Frequently obeisance will be made from a sitting position; in this case, and when standing, it consists of holding the palms of the hands together in front of the face and bowing the head in the familiar Indian attitude of reverence.

The chanting of the Pali verses then begins.[2] These consist of traditional well-known forms of homage to the Buddha, the Dharma and the Sangha, usually beginning with the 'Namo':

'Namo tassa bhagavato arahato sammāsambuddhassa!'

'Homage to the Blessed One, the Exalted One, the Fully-Enlightened One!' The leader begins by saying in Pali:

'The Blessed One who is far from desire — I worship that Blessed One, the Lord Buddha'. At this point he bows once.

[1] As Bhikshu Sangharakshita points out, this daily office is something that the Mahāyāna has inherited from the Hīnayāna. 'Flowers, lights and incense had been offered to the Buddha even during his lifetime and sins confessed to him.' Some of the formulas used in the daily office, he adds, 'are as old as Buddhism itself' (op. cit., p. 446).

[2] In much of what follows use has been made of information provided by Dr. K. E. Wells, both in conversation in Rangoon, and in his book, *Thai Buddhism* (Bangkok, 1960).

'The holy Dharma which the Blessed One proclaimed —
I worship that holy Dharma', and he bows again.

'The Sangha, the disciples of the Blessed One, who have
kept the precepts well — I bow to the holy Sangha', and he
bows a third time. He then says, 'Let us join in praise of the
excellence of the Buddha', and the assembly proceeds to
chant in unison the Buddhabhithuti:

> The Tathāgata Lord who is far from desire is one whom
> we should worship and adore. He is the self-enlightened
> who has achieved the ultimate in wisdom and upward
> striving. He attained bliss [or Nibbana] and omniscience.
> He taught those who were teachable, no one more than he.
> He was the teacher of devatās and men. He achieved bliss.
> He proclaimed the Dharma, making it clear with his own
> supreme wisdom. He taught this world together with all
> the devatās [celestial beings] māras [devils] Brahmas, and
> all creatures including ascetics, brahmanas and men. He
> proclaimed the Dharma which is sweet [melodious] in its
> beginning, sweet in the middle portion, and sweet in its
> conclusion. He proclaimed ascetic conduct [*brahmacaraya*]
> in its entirety, in its ramifications and in all purity. We
> reverently adore that Blessed Lord. We give highest
> adoration to that Blessed Lord.

Similar chants in praise of the Dharma and the Sangha then
follow together with other verses in salutation of the 'Three
Gems', or affirming the adherence of the people to the Buddha
and his Dharma. Various chants are contained in handbooks
for the use of monks, and a great deal is left to the discretion of
the leader in the conduct of the service. The lay people do not
use anything corresponding to a prayer-book, but in the course
of time learn the verses by heart.

On *Uposattha* or 'sabbath' days the service will include a recitation of the eight moral precepts which the lay people undertake to observe, the people repeating each precept after the the monk who is leading the devotions. At the conclusion of this the monk adds: 'These eight precepts may you keep well as *Uposattha*, not being careless in any respect', and the congregation replies, 'Ama bhante', a response which is roughly equivalent to the Jewish–Christian 'Amen' — so be it.

The layman who wishes to observe Uposattha strictly will remain within the monastery for the rest of the day and night, fasting from midday onwards.

BUDDHIST FESTIVALS IN SOUTH-EAST ASIA

The festivals of the Buddhist calendar provide further occasions for devotional services similar to those which have been described. Festival days in South-East Asia are, like red-letter days in Catholic Europe, occasions which concern the whole community: houses are decorated, and there are processions through the town or village with music and a good deal of pageantry. The most outstanding is Vesak, which is celebrated at the full moon in May, and commemorates three events of outstanding importance for Buddhists: the Buddha's birth, his enlightenment, and his entry into nirvana. The triple nature of the celebration can be traced back at least as far as the twelfth century. It is a temple or monastery-centred festival, with open-air processions, often at dusk, with lighted candles. In Thailand there is a royal procession in which all the members of the king's family take part and a service is conducted in the royal sanctuary by a senior monk. This, and the many other assemblies in temples and monasteries at Vesak, will often include a sermon in which the solemn significance of the festival is declared and set forth.

Another popular celebration of this kind is Magha Puja, which falls three months before Vesak, at the time of the full moon of February. This is a commemoration of the giving of the Patimokkha rules to the monks by the Buddha, and of his prophecy that he would enter nirvana three months from that time. It is sometimes referred to as the Buddhist All Saints Day, and, like Vesak, is a national holiday in most South-East Asian countries. In Bangkok there is a religious procession at dusk on the day of the full moon. This is known as the *wien tien* procession, which, says K. E. Wells, 'refers to the rite of circumambulation in which the participants carry candles and march in procession around a central object (i.e. a shrine), their right shoulders towards it. Sometimes this refers to a ceremony in which the participants form a circle, facing in, and in silence pass a candle from hand to hand. The candle is received with the right hand and passed on to the left, going three times around the circle. Each person holds the candle for an instant in both hands while he makes three circular motions in a vertical plane with it. Then with one hand he wafts the flame in the direction of the object of reverence.'[1]

Another important festival in South-East Asian countries is that which marks the end of the season of Lent, which is also the three months of the heaviest rains, the darkest time of the year in monsoon Asia. As the rains die away, and the air becomes dry and clear and sunny, there is a general mood of rejoicing. It is a time of the year much celebrated by Burmese poets. It falls during the seventh month of the Buddhist year, roughly in the October–November period. There are three main features of the festival. During Lent Buddhist monks are confined to their monasteries, apart from the morning rounds to collect food. At the end of this period, which has been specially devoted to study of the Dharma, there is a solemn congrega-

[1] K. E. Wells, *Thai Buddhism*, p. 72.

tion of the whole Sangha in each place, at which certain passages are recited from the Vinaya (the monastic rules), and each monk makes an act of confession. This solemn congregation is known as *Pavarana*, and attendance is obligatory for every monk. Each makes his act of confession, or, rather, the submitting of himself for correction by the other members of the Sangha, correction which may take the form of reproof and penance, or even expulsion from the Order. The second main feature of the festival is the presentation of new robes to the monks by the lay people. This ceremonial offering of robes is known as *Katina*. The third main feature is the decoration of every house, pagoda and building with lights, for three evenings from the eve of the full-moon day.

In Thailand, according to Wells, there are special services of devotion at the temples, which are usually crowded, and at night 'the yards and verandas of the homes of the devout are illuminated by candles, tiny oil lamps, or latterly, by coloured electric lights. The temples are likewise illuminated, and small boys cheerfully assist in placing candles about the bases and high up on the sides of the cetiyas (pagodas). While the candles flicker in the night air men and women may be seen kneeling before the cetiyas, palms of hands together, reciting the *Namo* and favourite Pali gāthās'.[1]

It is this ritual element in Theravada Buddhism (of which the reader has been provided with a few brief glimpses), which, of the important place it holds in the Buddhist life and culture of South-East Asia, renders false the comparison which is sometimes made between Theravada Buddhism and Protestant Christianity. Some Theravadin monks, it is true, may seem to be excessively preoccupied with the precise words of the Buddha in the Pali canon, and by itself this could undoubtedly lead to an unrelieved dogmatism. But generally it never is 'by

[1] K. E. Wells, op. cit., pp. 103 ff.

itself'. Emphasis upon the text of scripture is balanced in the
day-to-day life of the religion by the effect of the ritual practices
and the discipline of meditation. It is this combination of
scriptural and devotional or ritual elements which gives the
Theravada its characteristically Buddhist religious quality.
That is to say, the kind of religious life in which it is taken for
granted that theological argument is no substitute for spiritual
experience, and that without regular, disciplined devotion and
ritual practice, theology becomes mere ideology, the enemy of
true religion and of the holy life.

The large place which ceremonies and festivals have in
Buddhist life is significant for others than Buddhists. The fact
that this is found even in so apparently agnostic a system as
Theravada Buddhism reveals an impulse towards worship
which is the more remarkable in that it occurs in a system
which might in theory have been thought to preclude worship.
But spiritual seriousness seems to require devotional practice —
even where it might least be expected. What is more, one cannot doubt that such religious observances have had a great deal
to do with maintaining the strength of Buddhism and its
appeal to the people of these countries. In the light of this it is
possible to suggest that Buddhism may have disappeared from
India, its place of origin, because, among other reasons, it had
not provided itself with a context of popular, distinctively
Buddhist devotional practices. In India the lay supporters of
the Sangha appear to have remained largely Hindu in their
religious observances; they adhered either to the sacrificial
practices of Brahmanism, or found a more emotional outlet for
religious sentiment in the *bhakti* cults and were thus never fully
drawn into a Buddhist context of life and devotion.

BUDDHISM AS RELIGION:
GENERAL CONCLUSIONS

What is certain, so far as the Buddhism of contemporary Asia is concerned, is that what Western religion calls 'sacramentals' play no little part. The kind of Buddhism which is described in some academic textbooks on the subject, a dry and arid philosophy consisting of strings of abstract ideas and principles *only*, bears little resemblance to the Buddhism of Asia. This is most obvious in connection with popular devotional practices, some of which have been described in this chapter, but equally important elements in any total view of Buddhism are its missionary spirit, its monastic life, its shrines and images, its mythology, its continuing tradition of spiritual writings, its veneration of the masters of the spiritual life, the place given to these spiritual pioneers, the Buddha and the saints, but especially the Buddha, to whom veneration is offered by Buddhists as to no other mortal man. This is Buddhism, and this, unquestionably, is religion.

7

BUDDHISM'S RELIGIOUS RESISTANCE
TO SECULARISM

SOME observers might maintain that it is the 'religious' quality of Buddhism that is most likely to prove a weakness in the modern situation, and to affect adversely its ability to maintain its influence in the contemporary world. But to see the religious element in Buddhist culture as its area of weakness is, in the view of the present writer, a mistaken and superficial view of the matter. In fact, the recent history of the predominantly Buddhist countries of South-East Asia suggests that it is precisely their religious culture which offers the strongest resistance to Western secular materialism. It is therefore important that we should include here a brief review of that history.

BUDDHIST VALUES IN POST-WAR BURMA

On 2 March 1962 the Burmese government, headed by the devoutly Buddhist Prime Minister, U Nu, was swiftly and silently removed from office by a military coup. It happened in the small hours of the morning, and the whole operation was complete by the time most of the inhabitants of Rangoon began their day's work; it was done with the efficiency one had come to associate with the Army under General Ne Win. The event came as a surprise when it did, although it was not totally unexpected. Under U Nu's premiership Burma's political and economic difficulties had grown more and more acute until the point had been reached where in order to function at all as a modern state sterner measures seemed to be needed than those which had characterized the benevolent and pious rule of this self-declared champion of Buddhism.

It would be naïve to suggest that the issue was simply between a greater or lesser degree of Buddhist principle and practice in government policy. Obviously many other factors were involved in the army's taking over control of the country. Any Burmese national leader is likely to have experienced the same kind of difficulties that U Nu encountered, whether he was as pious a Buddhist or not. The new political *élite* lacked the skills necessary to adapt Western forms to the Burmese situation,[1] they had to contend with complicated internal struggles and with the opposition of strong traditional elements in Burmese society. U Nu has been seen by some observers as a type of leader not without parallel in other newly emerging nations, especially in Africa, the leader who is charismatic but inexperienced. It is because he was so avowedly *Buddhist* an administrator that the difficulties into which his government ran might be taken to indicate some conflict between Buddhist principles and the political and economic factors at work in the twentieth-century world. It is therefore worth noting that successive governments of independent post-war Burma have gone to the trouble of denying that there is any incompatibility between the philosophy of Buddhism, and the aims of a

[1] See Manning Nash, 'Southeast Asian Society', *Journal of Asian Studies* (May 1964), p. 421.

socialist welfare-state. The official position of U Nu's government in this respect was stated thus: 'The new Burma sees no conflict between religious values and economic progress. Spiritual health and material well-being are not enemies: they are natural allies.'[1] And in similar terms the revolutionary government of Ne Win, in a statement of its official policy, made in March 1963, placed equal emphasis upon both the spiritual and the material life of man, and condemned what it called 'dogmatic views of vulgar materialism'.[2] But such declarations could be regarded as indicating that an attempt is being made to hold together in the contemporary life of Burma what are in fact irreconcilable elements of thought and practice. As a Burmese economist working in the United States has put it, 'whether or not the political leadership can correlate the traditional cultural values to the modern socialist environment in actual policy implementation is for the future to see.'[3] Certainly, traditional cultural values and socialist aims both received their fair share of attention from U Nu's government. Cultural values mean, in Burma, largely Buddhist values, and during the Nu régime special courts were set up so that the monks might carry out the affairs of the Order in a way that had not been possible under British rule, Pali studies received official encouragement, a 'Sasana' (or religious) Council was set up to deal with all matters relating to religion, the Sixth World Buddhist Council was convened at Rangoon, a new pagoda and conference hall in the shape of a huge artificial 'cave' were built at public expense, and — the measure for which perhaps Nu's premiership is best remembered by

[1] *Pyidawtha, The New Burma* (Rangoon, 1954), p. 10.

[2] Brian Crozier, 'The Communist Struggle for Power in Burma', *The World Today* (March 1964), p. 110.

[3] Mya Maung, 'Cultural Values and Economic Change in Burma', *Asian Survey* (March 1964), p. 764.

Buddhists — Buddhism was made the official state religion. On the other hand socialist aims were equally vigorously pursued. The three main points in government plans and conferences for the development of Burma were declared to be nationalization, Burmanization and industrialization. The last of these means for Burma 'to get the things of the modern world now, fast'![1]

Not surprisingly, therefore, even under U Nu's paternalism, one heard complaints from serious and responsible senior monks about the difficulties which the Buddha's religion had to face in the modern situation. Like U Nu's government, that of Ne Win is socialist in its political aims and methods, but it seems to pursue these more relentlessly and single-mindedly than did its predecessor. The unease and anxiety felt by some Buddhist monks, even under U Nu's rule, is not likely to diminish under the Army régime. But is this unease perhaps not so much the symptom of an unsatisfactory relationship with the political powers as the result of the increasingly secular and materialist character of modern life, in which Burma is inevitably involved and to which she cannot, any more than any other state, remain immune? Is it in other words a symptom of the long-term, basic difficulty of *correlating* Buddhist cultural values and materialistic aims? Government policy statements denying that there is in Burma any conflict between *traditional* religion and economic progress might thus be thought to be more in the nature of a pious hope than a genuinely critical appraisal of the contemporary situation.

That there is a certain element of tension between Buddhist principles on the one hand, and the practical policies of successive post-war governments of independent Burma is possible, but this has to be seen in proper perspective. For there is also a very clear repudiation of Western culture and ideals which shows itself frequently and at every level of Burmese

[1] Manning Nash, op. cit., p. 423.

society. The use of English is discouraged, in spite of its value
as a medium of higher education, and the use of Burmese is
urged in every quarter. Very few Burmans wear Western
dress; even the small (and now diminishing) number of
British and American educated intellectuals prefer the traditional Burmese costume. These are only superficial indications of
a xenophobia that runs deep, even into the life of Rangoon. On
attaining independence from British rule in 1948 Burma opted
out of membership of the Commonwealth, and has stayed out.
While there is more to Burmese xenophobia than simply
negative anti-Western feeling the latter constitutes a very strong
part of it. And on the other hand, the positive element is the
desire to maintain and defend Burmese culture, which means,
in effect, Buddhist culture. There is in Burma a well-known
and widely accepted saying, 'To be Burmese is to be Buddhist'.

The fact that the Burmese government has accepted the
necessity for *industrialization* has to be seen in close conjunction
with the other two main aims of government policy —
nationalization (understood as the social ownership of the means
of production and distribution) and *Burmanization*. It is
arguable, and it has in fact been argued, that the improvement
of the economic condition of the peasants and workers which
it is hoped the nationalizing and industrializing of Burma's
economy will bring about will facilitate the pursuit of Buddhist
ideals by the people, by freeing them from the burden of great
poverty. A foreign observer of the Burmese scene in 1964 noted
'the Government's careful policy towards the Buddhist monks',
for, as he commented, it is they who 'keep Burmese society
going'.[1] And as we shall see more clearly in connection with
Marxism in Burma, whenever in the clash of economic and
social policies nakedly materialistic attitudes are recognized
Burma's Buddhist politicians unhesitatingly denounce them.

[1] 'Nationalism in Burma', *The Times* (London, 13 Feb. 1964), p. 13.

Such denunciation would not in itself necessarily mean very much, but for the fact that in such cases the politician is aware of the pressure of Buddhist opinion behind him.

BUDDHIST VALUES IN THAILAND

When we turn to consider Thailand it might be thought that since this is a country which has for some time been relatively prosperous by Asian standards at least, the Thai people would tend to be materialistic in outlook. But here also Buddhist ideals are the determining factor. David A. Wilson sums up the situation admirably: 'Although it would be false to depict the Thai as uninterested in the acquisition of wealth, he puts great value on the accumulation of merit and on the making of merit through doing good in the infinite ways that good may be done. The most direct manner of merit-making is to participate in, and support, the faith. Thus a man's greatest opportunity to make merit is to become a monk and a woman's is to support a man in this endeavour. The monk's life, in fact and symbol, is the mode of most merit and greatest value. It demonstrates the total denial of things of this world. The monk's role — celibate, half-starved, dressed in torn robes, and living as a mendicant — is a respected and valued symbol of the denial of desire, Buddhism's greatest value.'[1] As Wilson points out, it is the Buddhist pattern of ideas and values which in Thailand 'forms the ethical pattern of national behaviour'.[2] It is highly significant that this continues to be the case in a country which, while remaining free from European rule throughout the modern period, has by no means been isolated from contacts with the West, and has sent its young people to many of the

[1] *Marxism in Southeast Asia*, ed. F. N. Trager (Stanford University Press, 1960), p. 69.
[2] Ibid.

universities of Europe and America. Yet in spite of such contacts, as well as the presence in Thailand of American and European missionaries, what has to be noted is 'the failure of any other ideology [than Buddhism] to make a real penetration into the Thai *Weltanschaung*'.[1]

BUDDHIST VALUES IN CEYLON

In Ceylon the encounter of Buddhism with a materialistic way of life is again an aspect of the encounter with Western culture, here experienced on a broader front, over a longer period and at much closer terms than in either Burma or Thailand. Throughout the whole of the nineteenth century Ceylon was subject to European rule, and in fact even from the sixteenth century onwards was exposed to European influences to a greater degree than any other country in Asia. First under the Portuguese, then under the Dutch, and finally, from 1815, under the British, Ceylon has undergone a very thorough exposure to Western ideas and ways of life.

It is remarkable that the effect of this upon the traditional Buddhist culture of Ceylon has not been greater than it in fact has. At the beginning of the period of European invasion Buddhism was in a somewhat lethargic condition in the island — considerably less vigorous than it is today. Yet after four centuries of European influence only 9 per cent of the population has embraced the religion of the West, and this in spite of heavy Portuguese Catholic 'incentives' and, later on, Protestant missionary zeal. Under Portuguese rule the pressure upon the Ceylonese to become Roman Catholics was often inescapable. Under Dutch rule also it was often found safer to conform to Christian customs. During the period of British administration the pressure was more subtle: Western educa-

[1] Ibid.

tion was the passport to a good position, and such education was largely in the hands of Western missionary organizations. Yet after these four centuries of religious and cultural persuasion of various kinds there is still a resistance amounting to 91 per cent of the population, and more than two-thirds of this is Buddhist.

But perhaps one ought to ask what effect this encounter has had upon traditional Buddhist culture and values. During the period of colonial rule there was undoubtedly a strong tendency for those Ceylonese who were able to imitate European ways and accept European standards. For even Christian missionaries brought more than Christianity to Ceylon; they imported their own Western living standards, institutions, and social behaviour. In fairness it must be said that it was difficult for them to avoid doing so, because of the number of other Europeans in the island — traders, tea-planters, government servants and so on. Christianity's contacts with Buddhism in Ceylon have suffered from the fact that it has been the official religion of commercial and imperialistic nations possessed of military power.

It may be objected that the linking of Western materialism with Christianity in this way is a mistaken view of things, and a misrepresentation of the latter. Nevertheless the two have been closely connected in the eyes of the people of Ceylon. In particular, it is the influence of Christian schools which is fastened upon by those who are concerned with restoring or maintaining traditional Buddhist values. For Buddhist children who were scholars in Christian schools were, indirectly if not directly, made to despise their own religion and culture. 'In this country now, although there is no visible foreign yoke in the form of a colonial government we are as subject as we were before we broke loose from the British bonds a few years ago, to the invisible yoke of evil, unenlightened teachings, practices, habits, customs and views, fostered by the British. Thus we are still in moral bondage to the West.'[1]

On the other hand W. H. Wriggins comments on the report of the Buddhist Committee of Enquiry[2] that it 'urged upon the wealthy a puritanical simplicity of life worthy of early Calvinist preachers as a means for furthering development'.[3] As he points out, Buddhist culture does not mean the exclusion of all concern for matters affecting the economic condition of the people, and there are notable historical examples of the vigorous promotion by Buddhist rulers of works for the public good.[4]

What there has been in Ceylon in modern times is a notable reaction among Buddhists *against* the kind of civilization in which monetary values are the supreme criterion of success or achievement, and in which private wealth can be regarded as a sign of divine favour. This is all the more remarkable in view of the fact that Ceylon is not an impoverished nation, and has in fact a considerable wealth of natural resources. Ceylon's Buddhists, in questioning the pursuit of material prosperity as the main aim of life, are not doing so in any mood of sourness or jealousy, but rather from considered and deliberate choice. Here is a country to which Nature has been very kind, and which could well be described as flowing with milk and honey, whose Buddhist scholars and leaders, laymen as well as monks, are prepared to affirm, and to act upon the affirmation, that there are higher aims in life than doubling one's standard of living within the next twenty-five years.

[1] Editorial, 'True Freedom', *Buddha Jayanti*, 13 Aug. 1954. Vol. i, nos. 16, 17. Quoted by W. H. Wriggins, *Ceylon: Dilemmas of a New Nation* (Princeton University Press, 1960), p. 202.

[2] *The Betrayal of Buddhism* (Balangoda, 1956).

[3] *Ceylon: Dilemmas of a New Nation* (Princeton, 1960), p. 209.

[4] Ibid.

But, as we have already noted, this does not mean that the Buddhist of Ceylon goes to the opposite extreme and has no concern for the proper ordering of human affairs. As in Burma, here too it is recognized that the provision of the necessities of life for everyone is a legitimate area of Buddhist concern. Dr. G. P. Malalasekera, one of Ceylon's leading scholars and diplomats, put it thus: 'It is not a matter of indifference to the Buddhist whether this human "civilization" succeeds or fails. He must make it succeed because he is involved in it. The Buddhist ideal is that the spiritually developed man strives to bring liberation and happiness not only to himself but to *all* beings without exception. . . .'[1] The only thing that Buddhism can never be is a *private* affair, since in the Buddhist view there are no private individuals. The aim of Buddhism is inherently *social* in its concern; it is to bring all men to nirvana; this objective concerns society as a whole.

BUDDHIST CONCERN FOR THE MATERIAL WORLD

It must not be assumed therefore, that because there is a tendency among modern Buddhists in Asia to reject the materialistic values of secular Western society, Buddhism can be accused of indifference towards the so-called 'material' realm. Materialism consists in the mistake of thinking that there are solid material substances and that reality resides in them, and in them alone, and that all else is epiphenomenal superstructure. Basically, this is the assumption that underlies the popular materialism of the West. In the opinion of some Christians, Eastern thought makes the opposite mistake: 'in order to safeguard both the reality and the supremacy of spirit, it

[1] 'The East and West and Buddhism', *The Middle Way*, xxxiii, no. 4, p. 157.

dismisses the material as illusory.'[1] The result of this exclusion of the material, it is said, is an 'uncontrolled empire of matter', for 'you cannot regulate what you do not recognize. If matter is so unreal that spirit, which is real, has neither need for it nor control of it, then in its own sphere it will make havoc'.[2]

Perhaps the real trouble here is the false dichotomy between the 'material' and the 'spiritual'. Any argument which starts from the assumption that there are two modes of being, the material and the spiritual, is now bound to seem pointless and irrelevant in view of the discovery by the physicist that there are no solid molecular 'substances' but something rather more like patterns of events. With this aspect of the matter, and the approximation of Buddhist and modern scientific ideas, we shall to some extent be concerned in a later chapter. Meanwhile it must be made clear that Buddhism does not result in an 'uncontrolled empire of matter'. What in common parlance is denoted by the word 'material' is referred to in Buddhist doctrine as the first of the five constituent elements of existence, and is called *rupa*, or form. The Buddhist attitude towards this 'material' aspect of existence is to make it serve the purpose of bringing enlightenment nearer: in other words to employ it in the characteristic ways it has been employed in Buddhist painting, sculpture, architecture and devotion (having recognized also that physical substances have their necessary role in maintaining man's life until enlightenment is reached — in other words, due and proper provision is made for the use of the physical as sustenance). No one who is aware of the extent of Buddhist art, literature, and all that is comprehended in the term 'Buddhist culture' could seriously maintain that Buddhism involves contempt for the material world. The real points at issue between Buddhism and secular materialism concern the

[1] Archbishop William Temple, *Nature, Man and God* (London, 1949), p. 36.
[2] Ibid.

aim and purpose of human life, and the use to be made of material things. For the secularist, the aim of life appears to be the acquiring and the enjoyment of 'consumer goods'. This attitude is one which insidiously communicates itself even to those in the West who adhere to a religious tradition which is basically opposed to it, and who are warned against it in the words of Christ: 'Take heed, and beware of all covetousness; for a man's life does not consist in the abundance of his possessions.'[1] Buddhists are now increasingly confronted by the same tendency, but there are signs that Buddhist culture is somewhat more resistant to the establishment of the acquisitive society.

One of the areas of life where modern developments do constitute a serious challenge to a traditional Buddhist culture is the *urbanization* which is an essential part of industrialization, and the social changes which this brings about. This demands of Buddhism, it is now beginning to be realized by some leaders of Buddhist thought, a new working out, for mid-twentieth century, of a Buddhist theory of society and an expounding of the Buddhist ethic in terms of a contemporary pluralist society.

It is at this point that a consideration of the Buddhist encounter with Marxism in the modern world is particularly relevant, and to this we now turn.

[1] Luke xii. 15 (RSV).

Part Three

MARXISM
AND
RELIGION

8

BUDDHISM AND MARXISM:

HISTORICAL ENCOUNTER

BUDDHIST–MARXIST ENCOUNTER IN
SOUTH-EAST ASIA

DURING the period between the two World Wars, when Buddhist countries in Asia were under Western rule, nationalist leaders in those countries were often strongly attracted to Marxism. It is not difficult to see the reasons for this. In Burma many of the leaders in the movement for independence from British rule made their acquaintance with Marxist ideas while they were students at Rangoon University, largely through literature which had been brought from England. In his younger days U Nu used to translate portions of *Capital* and other Marxist works into Burmese for the Red Dragon Book Club, which aimed at a book a month for its circle of Burmese readers. Another of the same generation, Thein Maung, visited London in 1931, to be present as a representative of Burmese youth at the Round Table conference on the future of Burma. While he was there he met a number of Marxists and joined Palme Dutt's *Communist League against Imperialism*. In these and similar ways Marxist ideas made their way from London to Rangoon during the twenties and thirties.

What appealed to these young Burman Buddhists in the

writings of Marx and Engels was not so much the doctrine of historical materialism, but the criticism by Marx of the grossly materialistic capitalism of the West. It was the attack on this kind of materialism which appealed to young Asians, especially when such materialism was seen masquerading as something else — i.e. putting up a smoke-screen of moralistic Christianity to hide its own ugly nature — and when it was characterized as a materialism which allowed the few by their selfish operation of the economy to dominate and exploit the many. What Marx sought, they believed, was a materialism of a different kind, one which was directed and controlled by man for the good of man. The change which he sought to bring about was that to which he challenged his contemporaries everywhere in the last of his Theses on Feuerbach: 'The philosophers have only interpreted the world in various ways; the point, however, is to change it.' The characteristically Marxist emphasis on the idea that human beings are determined by their environment, and especially by economic factors, and that art, philosophy, religion and ethics are simply the superstructure raised above the economic realities — this view was passed over fairly lightly by these young Burmese nationalists. The Marxism which they hailed as an ally was seen as a new intellectual weapon aimed against the economic systems of the West, which, in their external relations with Asian and African countries, were necessarily imperialistic because they were capitalist.

But there was a further reason in the circumstances of the time for an alliance of Buddhists and Marxists. In Burma, in the inter-war period, the movement for national independence had not only a Marxist colouring, it was also very strongly Buddhist-inspired. This was because British rule in Burma had failed to make provision for a *Sangharāja*, or national head of the Buddhist monastic order, of the kind that had existed in pre-

British days under the Burmese kings. British policy was intended to be one of religious neutrality, and to avoid involvement in Buddhist affairs. It was regarded by the Burmese, however, as having the positively harmful effect of preventing the Buddhist Sangha from functioning properly. In this way, rightly or wrongly, British rule actively antagonized Buddhist Burma, so that among the most vigorous leaders of the struggle to rid the country of alien rule were Buddhist monks, such, for example, as U Wisera, who fasted to death in the furtherance of this cause. His statue, which stands in a prominent position now on a main road in Rangoon, bears witness to the part played by Buddhist monks in the struggle against foreign rule, a struggle in which Buddhists found that Marxists were their allies.

Once independence had been achieved, however, the apparent common ground between them seemed to disappear. The government of independent Buddhist Burma was more Fabian socialist than Marxist in complexion. The generation of leaders who, as students, had flirted with Marxism, now that they were responsible for the governing of a Buddhist country found themselves confronted more clearly with the issues that divided the two systems of thought. Distinction between Buddhism and Marxism began to be made, with varying degrees of sharpness. Some differentiated between Communism and Marxism, expressing their distrust of the former. Burmese Buddhist leaders such as U Nu came in for criticism from Moscow because of their policy towards Burmese Communists.[1]

Already in the post-war period, even before the achievement of independence, Burmese Communists had clashed with the Buddhist sentiments of the majority of the people. In December 1945 an attack on Buddhism by a Communist writer, Thakin Thein Pe, called forth such strong protests from the Rangoon

[1] See *Bulletin of the Institute for the Study of the USSR* (April 1956).

press that he was forced to apologise.[1] Another incident occurred a few months later when 'some communist students of Rangoon University violated the sacred Shwedagon Pagoda with placards deriding the omniscience of the Buddha'.[2] Again there was a public outcry, and after this the Communists of Burma learnt to observe a proper respect, in public at least, towards things Buddhist. So well did they learn this lesson of the importance of Buddhism in Burma that at the April 1956 election the successful Communist candidates presented their electoral deposit money for the purchase of Buddha images.[3]

Such was the nature of Burmese feeling about Communism that even U Nu, greatly respected leader that he was, was forced by strong criticism from fellow-Buddhists to withdraw a proposal which he had made, as part of a policy for appealing to left-wing elements, for a league for the 'propagation of Marxist doctrines' which would 'read, discuss and propagate the writings of Marx, Engels, Lenin, Stalin, Mao Tse-tung, Tito, Dimitrov and other apostles of Marxism'.[4] This was in 1948. By 1950, in introducing the *Buddha Sāsana* Organization Act in the Burmese parliament, which was intended, he said, 'to lay solid and lasting foundations of Buddhism' in Burma, he hastened to add that this was not in any way intended to disparage other religions, but rather, 'to combat effectively anti-religious forces.'[5] By the latter, as he went on to make clear, he meant Communism. 'It will be our duty to retort in no uncertain terms that the wisdom or knowledge that might be

[1] See Richard Adloff and Virginia Thompson, *The Left Wing in Southeast Asia* (New York, 1950), p. 91.

[2] Ibid.

[3] See G. Fairburn, 'Aspects of the Burmese Political Scene', *Pacific Affairs*, vol. 29 (1956), p. 213.

[4] R. Butwell, *U Nu of Burma* (Stanford, California, 1963), pp. 97 f.

[5] Hugh Tinker, *The Union of Burma* (London, 3rd edn. 1961) p. 169.

attributed to Karl Marx is less than one-tenth of a particle of dust that lies at the feet of our great Lord Buddha.'[1]

Another Burmese political leader, U Ba Swe, took a slightly different view. In a speech delivered in 1951 he said, 'The acceptance of Marxism does not necessarily make one a Communist. To be a Communist you have to observe certain set rules of conduct. Especially the so-called Communists believe that to become a Communist one must unequivocally accept Soviet leadership.' Concerning Marxism he went on to argue that it was in his view complementary to Buddhism: 'Marxist theory deals with mundane affairs and seeks to satisfy material needs in life. Buddhist philosophy, however, deals with the solution of spiritual matters. . . .'[2] He ended his speech with the claim that his study of Marxism had only strengthened his Buddhist convictions, and that the two systems were ultimately in harmony. On the other hand, U Nu quite clearly dissociated himself from Marxism of any variety in a speech which he made at a political congress in 1958: 'When we were younger, we had not yet studied Marxism in detail and in all its aspects. Neither did we know Buddhism in detail or with any exactness. At that time, more or less on hearsay and cursory reading, we impetuously loudly proclaimed that Marxism was the same as Buddhism. We are very remorseful for having made, at one time, such ill-considered and unfounded claims.'[3]

Later in the same year in which U Nu made this speech internal affairs in Burma had become so chaotic that the army, under General Ne Win, were forced to intervene and take over the government of the country. Then, in 1960, after a brief period of more efficient administration, the army handed the

[1] Tinker, op. cit., p. 170.

[2] U Ba Swe, *The Burmese Revolution* (Rangoon, 1952), pp. 6 f.

[3] Reported in *The Nation* (Rangoon), 30 January 1958; quoted by Butwell, op. cit., p. 28.

reins back to the politicians; a general election was held and
U Nu was returned as prime minister. But by the beginning of
March 1962 the state of affairs, economically and politically,
was just as bad if not worse than before, and Ne Win and the
Army again stepped in, but this time it was clearly not as a
temporary measure.

Events since 1962 have led some observers to conclude that
what has taken place in Burma has been, in all but name, a
Marxist revolution, although of an independent, Tito-ist kind.
The banks have been nationalized, and so has most retail
trading. Parliamentary democracy has been shelved, and the
legal system has been seriously interfered with. In 1965 all
private schools throughout the country, whether run by
Burmese or foreign agencies, were taken over by the government. There are Marxists of the Soviet persuasion in the
administration over which Ne Win presides. Army officers
have been issued with reading lists of books by such authors as
Marx, Engels, Lenin, Stalin, Bertrand Russell, G. D. H. Cole,
J. Strachey and Jayaprakash Narayan.

All this might seem to mean that the Buddhist rule of U Nu
has been replaced by the virtually Marxist regime of Ne Win.
There are other factors to be taken into account, however.[1]
Communism in Burma is of two kinds, underground and
above-ground, or proscribed and permitted. The underground
variety are the guerillas (known as the Burma Communist
Party) who since 1963 at least have firmly followed the Peking
line. The violence which they advocate, and practise, accords
with the Chinese Communist view of Marxist revolution. It is
worth noting that Ne Win's army coup in 1962 was virtually
bloodless; the only death was that of a schoolboy who was shot
by accident. The underground BCP has its contacts among the

[1] See Brian Crozier, 'The Communist Struggle for Power in Burma', *The
World Today*, March 1964.

students at Rangoon University, and the student assessment of Ne Win's régime as a 'fascist military dictatorship' was quickly confirmed by the BCP politburo.[1] In the light of this student-BCP connection should perhaps be seen the unusual violence which erupted in August 1962 when a number of students were killed by Army action on the campus of Rangoon University.

The above-ground Communists are the Union Workers Party; these follow the Soviet line and are said to be Soviet-supported. In Russia's struggle with China for influence among the uncommitted countries the policy has been one of encouraging 'national democratic fronts' in which Communists can work with socialists in countries where the policy is anti-capitalist but not fully communist. In the light of this must be seen the fact that pro-Soviet UWP Communists have taken office in Ne Win's administration.

How Marxist does this make the present Burmese government? An answer may be found in the fact that while Moscow approved of the economic measures taken by Ne Win (which were mentioned above) there were serious reservations about some of the passages in the statement of the army government's 'philosophy' which was published in 1963 — especially those in which 'some so-called leftists' are condemned for 'their dogmatic views of vulgar materialism'.[2]

One can say that the difference between U Nu's policy and that of the Ne Win régime is that the latter is not so much anti-religious, as *anti-traditional*.

For while it has condemned materialism, the Ne Win régime has not hesitated, on the other hand, to reverse measures passed by U Nu's government which enhanced the traditional

[1] Crozier, op. cit., pp. 108 ff.
[2] *The System of Correlation of Man and His Environment* (The Philosophy of the Burma Socialist Programme Party) (Rangoon 1963), p. 34.

aspects of Burmese Buddhism. The decree making Buddhism the State religion was cancelled, although this decree had been regarded by U Nu and the traditionalists as the most important achievement in Burmese affairs of the last decade. The General Council and the Executive of the Buddha Sasana (Religion) Council was dissolved by Ne Win, and the observance of the Buddhist Sabbath was discontinued. The latter action, particularly, could be interpreted as a sign of Ne Win's primary motive being a desire to modernize Burmese life, for the closing of government offices and post offices on a different day of the week each time (the Buddhist Sabbath is governed by the phases of the moon) had meant a certain amount of confusion in the business community.

At the time of writing the indications are that Ne Win's rule does not mean the acceptance of Communism or the rejection of Buddhism. Both the methods and the aims of Communism have been rejected. What has been affirmed is a socialist theory of the State. The end in view seems to be a national culture combining the tenets of both Buddhism and socialism, for socialist theory is seen to be in accord with Buddhist principles, and, without any need for subtle exegesis, derivable from them. The egalitarian nature of Burmese society is one result of Burma's Buddhist culture. Another is the rejection of the private-profit motive. This is explained in the new government's 'philosophy' by the use of the Buddhist concepts of *lobha*, or greed, and deviation from ethical conduct (*sila*). But such exposition is hardly necessary. Buddhist Burma is traditionally a non-acquisitive society. Burmese culture discourages thrift and hence, the accumulation of capital; economists discern an 'inhibition against acquisitiveness'.[1] Those professions and callings are more highly esteemed which 'are not so

[1] Mya Maung, 'Cultural Values and Economic Change in Burma', *Asian Survey* (March 1964), pp. 759 f.

conspicuously acquisitive and deviant from the traditional norms'.[1] Burmese Buddhist society, that is to say, is essentially non-capitalistic in nature. In the long-term view, U Nu's government and Ne Win's are pursuing the same ends, because they start from the same premises in Burmese Buddhism. It is this, more than any other single factor, which explains how Burma comes to travel the road to socialism. And it is equally Buddhism which is responsible for Burma's refusal to travel that other road which for a number of reasons might have seemed attractive — the road to totalitarian Communism.

The story of Ceylon's encounter with Marxism is very similar to that of Burma. In the early 1930's Ceylonese students at London University met with Marxists, absorbed their doctrines, and were attracted to Marxism both because of what seemed to them its relevance to the then dismal state of capitalist society in Britain during the years of economic depression, and also because of its apparent sympathy with Asian nationalist aspirations. In London some of Ceylon's future political leaders met the leaders of the British Communist Party, and at the London School of Economics were considerably impressed by the brilliance of Harold Laski's Marxist analyses.[2] The movement which they formed in Ceylon on their return was inspired largely by hostility to British domination of their country. The subsequent history of that movement is not our concern here. It is sufficient to say that although conditions in Ceylon were by no means unfavourable to Marxism, especially during the struggle for independence and the years immediately following, the left wing movement in Ceylonese politics never went to great extremes, nor did Marxist ideas make any great impression on the Ceylonese people as a whole. Marxism has remained a minority movement in Ceylon. In the low country, especially in the west of the island, where Marxist candidates

[1] Ibid.   [2] See W. H. Wriggins, op. cit., p. 124.

enjoy the support of Buddhists at election time, this is as much because they are anti-Catholic as for any positive attraction in their policies. It is significant also that there is a prominent Trotskyite element among Ceylon's Marxists, an element which is repulsed by the violence and totalitarianism of Stalinist Russia. One of the main Marxist groups, the Nava Lanka Sama Samaj Party (N.L.S.S.P.) was for many years severely critical of Stalin's 'betrayal' of Marxism, and, as Wriggins comments, this 'polemic against the excesses of Stalin's régime gave the N.L.S.S.P. an aura of being a democratic socialist party very much like the British Labour Party'.[1] Some of this similarity may be due to common origins; but one can see other reasons for it. In Ceylon, as in Burma, the ethos of Buddhism would produce an instinctive dislike of oppressive totalitarian bureaucracy. And, as in Burma, Buddhist culture (even though distorted and sometimes overlaid by Westernization) would produce a distrust of blatant acquisitiveness, with the result that in Ceylon all political parties are to some extent socialist. Any real danger in Ceylon of Communism's being able to establish itself by violence was probably in the period before 1950. Since then there has been a rise in the standard of living and the potential appeal of revolutionary Marxism has diminished. This has been accentuated in a traditionally religious country by the feeling that Communism is inevitably anti-religious.

In Thailand the influence of Marxism has been even slighter. Here, the dislike of foreign rule which in Burma brought Buddhists into temporary association with Marxists was quite lacking, since Thailand had not come under European colonial rule as other South-East Asian countries had. However, there is in Thailand, as in many of the lands of South Asia, a sizeable Chinese community, and among these there has been

[1] Op. cit., p. 132.

some interest in Communism. But the Chinese minority has not been allowed any legitimate part in Thai political life, and so any interest in Communism which they may have felt has perforce been focused on the achievements of the People's Republic of China.[1]

Moreover, the kind of social and economic situation which elsewhere has provided a fertile seed bed for the growth of a Communist party is not found in most of Thailand. No appeal can be made to class struggle, since in Thailand (as in Burma) the structure of society is at most one of gentle grading. There is no evident proletarian mass of workers or peasants living in subjection to an hereditary aristocracy (whether of blood or private wealth), and even between the upper and lower grades of society, such as they are, there is considerable social mobility.[2] Whether this kind of social structure is directly attributable to Buddhist culture or not, it is certainly favoured and strengthened by Buddhist ideas. If there is any one qualification for social distinction, it appears to be found in education, and in Thailand this is not the privilege of a few but is broadly based; again, this is partly the result of the traditional teaching function of the Buddhist monasteries which has produced a relatively high rate of literacy throughout the nation, as in Burma. Thailand's social structure is thus one which may best be described as a 'meritocracy' (whether this is understood in the Western or the Buddhist sense), and the achievement of merit is open to all. In Thailand there has been no less opportunity than in Ceylon and Burma for an encounter with Marxist ideas through foreign contacts, but there has been a less receptive audience. Where interest has been shown in Marxist ideas and literature, it has been among a few intellectuals, often those who have studied abroad. But interest in left-wing

[1] See David A. Wilson, 'Thailand and Marxism', in Trager, op. cit., p. 58.
[2] Wilson, op. cit., p. 63.

political thought has usually been an interest in democratic socialism rather than Communism.

What appears to be the one[1] notable exception to what has been said about Thailand's general lack of receptivity to communism is to be found in the north-east of the country. Here in the districts bordering Laos, remote from Bangkok, and for many years neglected by the government, there is greater poverty than in other parts of Thailand, and in recent years an increasing amount of Communist activity inspired largely by admiration for Ho Chi Minh, the North Vietnamese Communist President. Although Bangkok has known of this growth of Communist activity, the reports of General Sarit's régime on the subject were not seriously heeded, and it was believed that the government was crying wolf simply to justify certain policies of its own. It has now been seen that poverty, disaffection and a sense of kinship with the neighbouring Laos, have rendered the people of this area of Thailand much more open to Communist influence from North Vietnam and China than had been thought possible. 'The Communists do not have to march across the border: it is already dissolved. They do not ask the north-easterners to revolt against Bangkok, but only to identify themselves with their kin on the other side of the river, to promote a separatist movement based on their racial and cultural affinities.'[2]

Such a torrent of words has recently been poured out on the subject of Vietnam, that one hesitates to add anything. Our concern is limited to one aspect of the situation: the opposition of Buddhist monks and lay people to the various American-supported governments of South Vietnam has not been due to any alliance of Buddhism and Communism. Any common

[1] i.e. apart from the Malayan Communist Party leader, Chen Ping's sanctuary in southern Thailand.

[2] Denis Warner, *The Last Confucian* (Penguin Books, London, 1964), p. 279.

ground which may have appeared to have existed between the two has been largely accidental.

The point at which Buddhist leaders became involved in political disturbances was during the unfortunate Roman Catholic régime of the Diem family. The story begins with the incident on 8 May 1963 when Buddhists in Hue, the diocesan city of Archbishop Ngo Dinh Thuc, President Diem's elder brother, were forbidden by the government to fly the Buddhist flag at a time which happened to be one of the great festivals of the Buddhist year. From the hour when Buddhist crowds gathered to protest against this, and were fired upon by government troops the Buddhist leaders were drawn more and more into what was in effect political action against the Diem government. Relations between the Roman Catholic minority and the Buddhist majority of South Vietnam's population deteriorated. In June, as a matter of government policy, attacks were made by special military units on a number of Saigon pagodas. The Pope pleaded apparently in vain with Vietnam's Catholic rulers for an easing of the tension. By October the Ceylon representative at the United Nations raised the question of the oppression of Buddhists by the government of South Vietnam, and a U.N. fact-finding mission was sent to investigate. In this way Buddhist leaders in South Vietnam came to be the focus for popular anti-government feeling, but *quite distinct from* internal Communist insurgency. Once cast in this role, they continued to play it, even after the coup that brought the Diem régime to an end in November 1963. As a recent observer has put it: 'Accidents of history and circumstance have made "Buddhism" the focus and rallying symbol not only of political opposition to Catholic dominance but, more importantly, of inchoate nationalist aspirations.'[1]

[1] G. A. Carver, Jr., 'The Real Revolution in South Vietnam', *Foreign Affairs* (Washington, April 1965), p. 397. In general, Westerners have

It is not without significance that there is a tradition in South Vietnam which links Buddhism with nationalism and independence. The golden age of Buddhism in Vietnam was during the Ly dynasty, in the eleventh, twelfth and early thirteenth centuries. The rulers of this dynasty were themselves Buddhists and co-operated closely with the monastic orders. What is more thay are remembered for having successfully resisted Chinese encroachment in the north and for reducing Chinese political influence. 'Even in modern Vietnamese eyes they have a legendary aura, some of which extends to the Buddhist faith with which they were so intimately identified.'[1] In view of these traditions it is not easy to maintain the view that Buddhist monks in South Vietnam have been hand in glove with Chinese Communism.[2]

Nevertheless, the Roman Catholic Diem régime did accuse the Buddhist Sangha of providing a camouflage for Viet Cong infiltrators into South Vietnam. One can see how easily this could have happened — a man would need only to shave his head, and put on the orange robe of monkhood, and assume an appropriately humble demeanour in order to pass as a Buddhist monk. It is all the more remarkable, therefore, as John Mecklin records, that 'not a scrap of hard evidence of Communist penetration of the Buddhist (Sangha) turned up during the 1963 crisis'; and this, as he points out, 'despite frantic efforts by the Diem régime's considerable intelligence apparatus to find such evidence to discredit the Buddhists.' He adds that the intelligence service of the U.S.A. similarly tried and failed.[3]

---

underestimated Buddhist influence in Vietnam.   [1] Carver, op. cit., p. 395.

[2] For day by day, almost hour by hour records of events in which Buddhists were involved in opposition to the government in 1963 see Robert Scigliano, 'Vietnam: Politics and Religion', *Asian Survey* (Jan. 1964); and Denis Warner, *The Last Confucian*, ch. 13.

[3] John Mecklin, *Mission in Torment* (Doubleday, New York, 1965), p. 160.

Of the other countries of Asia in which Buddhism is found (apart from China and Tibet, which are to be dealt with separately) Japan is the outstanding case that has not yet been dealt with. But Japan cannot be classed as a predominantly Buddhist country in quite the same sense as Burma, Thailand, or even Ceylon. Buddhism and Shinto together have provided the main elements of Japanese culture, but it is the extent and the political power of Shinto in Japan, especially in the modern period up to the end of the Second World War, that has to some extent complicated the Buddhist–Marxist encounter there. Certainly the Communist Party has made little headway in Japan, largely because of the unfavourable internal and external circumstances. In pre-war, Imperial Japan Communism was outlawed. In the post-war period its lack of success has been very much bound up with the long-standing ill feeling between the Japanese and the Russians. The eventual repatriation in 1949 of about a million Japanese who had been taken prisoners by the Soviet Union in 1945 (in the last days of the war), and who had been held by the Russians until their plight became a matter of great public concern in Japan, is an example of this. The shock which was felt by their families and friends on their return, when it was found that the prisoners had been subjected to intensive Communist indoctrination, also had a profound effect on Japanese public opinion.[1]

It has to be remembered that there was not in Japan the same impulse to flirt with Marxism (as a gesture of anti-colonialism) that was felt, and expressed, in Burma and Ceylon under British rule, since in the pre-war period Japan was not subject to Western colonialism. But on the other hand it has to be noted that socialist ideas have met with fairly wide acceptance in Japan in modern times; some of this socialism has been of a more

[1] See John M. Maki, *Government and Politics in Japan* (London, 1962), pp. 173–8.

openly Marxist variety, some less so. Immediately after the second war the Japanese Socialist Party had sufficient popular support to be able to win a majority of seats in the 1947 general election.

There is therefore a certain parallel to be observed between largely Buddhist Japan and the predominantly Buddhist countries of South-East Asia, in that while Marxist socialism seems to have a certain appeal, it is Communism, especially because of its Russian association, that is vigorously resisted.

BUDDHIST–MARXIST ENCOUNTER IN THE U.S.S.R.

So far this survey of Buddhist–Marxist relations has been confined to predominantly Buddhist countries, and the reception which Marxist ideas and policies have had in such countries. The other aspect of the encounter between these two systems is to be seen in the U.S.S.R. and China, for these are countries in which the Marxist system predominates and Buddhism finds itself at best in a state of more or less tolerated coexistence. What has been the nature of the encounter in these countries?

The case of Buddhism in the U.S.S.R. is not particularly helpful as a normative example of the encounter between Buddhism and a Communist government, since Buddhism exists here only in certain Mongol republics, those of the Buryats, the Kalmyks and the Tuvinians.[1] Here Buddhism exists in a somewhat different form from that of South-East Asia; it was the variety which developed in Tibet which penetrated into these adjacent territories from the nineteenth century onwards. When it is recalled that it was the Tibetan Buddhists' 'ability to work magic which most impressed the Mongols'[2] one senses something of the kind of Buddhism

[1] For a general survey of Buddhism in the U.S.S.R. see W. Kolarz, *Religion in the Soviet Union* (London, 1961), ch. xiv.

[2] E. Conze, *A Short History of Buddhism* (Bombay, 1960), p. 110.

that existed in the Mongolian republics. Mongolian Buddhism was strongly institutional: some of the monasteries of Buryatia contained as many as a thousand inmates and possessed large areas of land. They were not only centres of learning and medical practice; they were also 'the political backbone of the Buryat–Mongol people'.[1] It was inevitable therefore that they should be the object of Communist hostility.

The history of Communist–Buddhist relationships in Russia falls into two periods, roughly divided by the year 1950, that is to say the time of the firm establishment of Communism in China, and the growth of U.S.S.R. interest in Asian affairs. During the earlier period the Buddhist peoples of the U.S.S.R. were fiercely persecuted. This persecution was both an expression of the general anti-religious policy of the Soviet Communists, and an attack on the dangerously strong institutional nature of Mongolian Buddhism, presenting as it did a serious hindrance to Communist social reconstruction. Anti-religious propaganda, carried out by the League of Militant Godless from the end of the twenties was, however, largely ineffective. This seems to have been due in part to its intellectually low level and its foolish excesses, and in part also to the way in which certain Buddhist leaders adapted themselves to the attack, outstanding among whom was Agvan Dordzhiev. This man, who had been tutor to the eighth Dalai Lama in Tibet, argued publicly and with great conviction that 'there was no conflict between Soviet power and Buddhism either on the ideological or on the practical political level'.[2] His argument on the ideological level seems to have been that Buddhism, like Marxism, was atheistic and scientific, and that there should therefore be no quarrel between them on that score. At the practical level he held that the continued existence of Buddhist

[1] Kolarz, op. cit., p. 450.
[2] Kolarz, op. cit., p. 455.

monasteries as centres of culture need present no opposition to the building of a socialist society. It is important to notice that Russian Communist hostility to Buddhism was in no way mollified by the claim to a common atheism. Such common ground was firmly denied. It was officially pointed out that 'Buddhist atheism has nothing to do with militant atheism based on the Marxist appraisal of the laws of nature and society'.[1] Nor did Soviet policy appear to pay any heed to the idea that the existence of Buddhist monasteries was compatible with a Communist society. From 1929 onwards one monastery after another was closed, until in 1937 the last remnants of the monastic system in Buryatia were destroyed. Most of the Lamas were imprisoned in concentration camps; some were executed. Dordzhiev himself died in prison in 1938.[2] According to Professor Poppe, 'nothing has been left of the Buddhist temples in Buryat–Mongolia and the land of the Kalmyks.'[3] He adds that the fate of Buddhism in the Soviet republics 'is a tragic example of the complete and wilful eradication of a religion'. On the other hand, however, during a visit to Moscow in 1960 Dr. Edward Conze saw some evidence of interest in Buddhist culture among intellectuals in the U.S.S.R. This consisted of a certain amount of academic work, the production of Russian translation of the *Dhammapada*, public lectures on Buddhist culture given by Dr. Malalasekera (then the Ceylonese ambassador) at the Lomonosov University, and a seminar of students engaged in the study of Pali. Conze mentions also the projected re-opening of the Lama temple in Leningrad. This last was said to be the result of representations made by Buddhist countries in Asia. Such a 'revival' of

---

[1] *Antireligioznik* (1930), no. 6, p. 66; quoted by Kolarz, p. 455.

[2] See N. Poppe, 'The Destruction of Buddhism in the U.S.S.R.' (*Bulletin of the Institute for the Study of the U.S.S.R.*, July 1956, pp. 14–20).

[3] Op. cit., p. 20.

interest in Buddhism could be regarded as largely a reflection of Soviet diplomatic interests in South Asia. Kolarz points out that since the firm establishment of Communism in China, Moscow has grown markedly more interested in co-operation with Asian countries, and has 'rediscovered what it had forgotten, namely, that the Buddhist community in the U.S.S.R. could have its propaganda uses'.[1] During the post-Stalin period especially there has been a severely limited revival of Buddhism in Buryatia also, exemplified in the re-establishment of two small monasteries, at Aga and Ivolga, at the latter of which the Chief Lama resides. During U Nu's visit to Moscow in 1955 the Chief Lama was brought to Moscow to meet this leader of the Burmese people, and was even given a place of honour at the receptions for U Nu at the Kremlin and the Burmese embassy. In conversation with the Burmese premier he was able to assure him, according to Soviet reports, that Buddhist monks and laymen in Russia 'fervently preserve the rites, dogmas and traditions of Buddhism'.[2]

A similar meeting between the next Chief Lama and the Ceylonese ambassador to the U.S.S.R. was held in Moscow in 1959, when again a favourable account was given of the condition of Buddhist community.[3] It appears however that such 'revival' of Buddhism is very carefully controlled by the Soviet authorities. Persecution of the Buddhist religion among the Kalmyk people had by 1939 almost entirely destroyed it, even before the Kalmyks were as a people deported to Siberia. Since their return to their original territory in 1957 one small monastery is reported to have reopened and a few Buddhist monks have appeared again in the villages, but 'local communist functionaries are closely watching their activities'.[4]

In Tuva, once a part of the Chinese empire, now an

[1] Op. cit., pp. 457 f. [2] Quoted by Kolarz, op. cit., p. 459.
[3] Kolarz, op. cit., p. 460. [4] Ibid., p. 464.

autonomous province of the U.S.S.R., the story has been in all essential respects the same, although here Buddhism was more closely associated with Shamanism, the original religion of this part of central Asia.

In the Mongolian People's Republic (the first country in Asia to become a socialist state) the undermining of Buddhism was soon begun with the help of Soviet advisers. In the ten years following 1930, when a Mongol League of Militant Godless was founded a campaign of increasing intensity and violence was carried on against what was until then virtually a Buddhist society of very similar kind to that of Tibet. This culminated in the trial and execution of large numbers of Lamas and a military offensive against the monasteries, in which tanks and aircraft were used. According to the reports of recent travellers in Mongolia, Buddhism survives there now only in a few remnants. Writing in 1958, Robert A. Rupen had this to say: 'While freedom of religion officially prevails and openly practising Buddhism can be found, the official (Buddhist) Church today operates in an extremely restricted and closely controlled manner. Most of the monasteries which have not been closed or completely destroyed serve secular purposes such as grain-storage or warehousing. Neglect threatens many fine Buddhist buildings.... The official Buddhist Church in Outer Mongolia today is a travesty, maintained mainly to impress foreigners and particularly for communist propaganda in other Buddhist countries of Asia.'[1]

Thus, so far as Soviet policy towards Buddhism is concerned, the most that can be said, even by one who is convinced that 'the ideals of communism and the ideals of Buddhism are in no way incompatible' is that 'the future cannot possibly be predicted'.[2]

[1] 'Inside Outer Mongolia', *Foreign Affairs*, vol. 37, no. 2, p. 332.

[2] E. Conze, 'Buddhism in the Soviet Union', *Middle Way*, vol. xxxv, no. 3, p. 114.

BUDDHIST–MARXIST ENCOUNTER IN CHINA

Many are the accounts of the condition of religion in China since the establishment of the People's Republic. Due allowance has always to be made for the extent to which these are coloured by the special interests of the reporter or observer, and whether he wears the rose-coloured spectacles of a sympathizer with the new régime or the dark glasses of dislike for all forms of socialism. On the whole it is probably true to say with regard to Buddhism (whatever may be the case with other religions) that it has not suffered any greater persecution or hostility under the People's Republic than it did under previous régimes; in some respects it may even have benefited from the change, and experienced something of a revival. Vocations to the monk-hood continue to be numerous, Buddhist associations have been formed which represent a strengthening of the Buddhist community, Buddhist publications and periodicals have increased, pilgrimages and religious ceremonies are attended by large numbers, and the government has taken in hand the restoration and reconstruction of temples that had been sadly neglected. All this is undoubtedly because it is recognized that Buddhism here is a *Chinese* religion.[1]

That is to say, Buddhism in China has the advantage, over Christianity for example, that it is not a foreign importation from the colonialist West, but is thoroughly Asian in origin and development. Buddhism may be said to have been one of the forms of popular religion in China ever since its introduction there from India towards the end of the second century of the Christian era. Its entry into China was not associated with military conquest, or the imposing of an alien culture; it won

[1] See André Migot, 'Le Bouddhisme en Chine', in *Présence du Bouddhisme* (Saigon, 1959), p. 712.

its way by adapting its doctrines to the Chinese environment and thus establishing its place as one of the religions of the country. It was popular, in the sense that it became widespread as a religion of the Chinese people, and has deeply affected Chinese culture. Opinions vary, however, on the subject of *how far* China can be regarded as Buddhist. Professor Zurcher, for instance, maintains that 'Buddhism, in the totality of Chinese culture, has always been a more or less marginal phenomenon', that is to say, 'it never played the role of a dominating creed, a *central* religious and philosophical tradition'.[1] This is true no doubt when comparison is being made with such Buddhist countries as Thailand, but it is equally true that Buddhism has had a deep effect on Chinese culture, especially in the south of China. Zurcher himself acknowledges, for example, that the popular stories of Buddhism 'actually formed the beginning of Chinese vernacular literature'.[2]

Buddhism was a popular religion also in the sense that it was despised by the Confucian literati, who regarded it as something foreign to the ancient civilization of China. It is important to remember that in general the rulers of China were traditionally Confucian. Emperors who favoured Buddhism were likely to encounter the hostility of the majority of the scholars and officials who adhered to the ethical system of Confucianism. Thus, 'the attitude of the imperial government had always been in theory rather contemptuous and hostile towards revealed religions',[3] and the attitude of the Communist rulers of China towards Buddhism, and towards other religions, is thus nothing new. The old Confucian attitude is now re-expressed in Marxist terms. As under the old régime,

[1] *The Legacy of China*, ed. R. Dawson (Oxford, 1964), p. 58.
[2] Op. cit., p. 69.
[3] C. P. Fitzgerald, *Flood Tide in China* (London, 1958), p. 159.

when religion was tolerated so long as it could be kept in check by the rulers, so it is also under the new. Professor Fitzgerald outlines the policy of the Communist Party in China towards all religions as follows:

'Religion is still widespread, but mass education will gradually weaken its hold. Religious schools are not permitted, religious instruction may only be given privately, or in a few permitted seminaries devoted to training priests and clergy. Churches, temples or mosques must be, as it were, licensed, exhibiting outside their gates a placard announcing that they are recognized places of worship for such and such a religion. Evangelization, open-air preaching, or any other activity likely to arouse popular interest and excitement are forbidden. No Church or religion must have any association with a foreign organization. Churches and religious organizations must no longer enter the educational field, must not run hospitals, orphanages or other institutions which would give them a character other than that of a strictly religious community devoted to worship and ritual, and to nothing else.'[1]

Nevertheless, Buddhism appears to enjoy a certain measure of favour in modern China, rather more than might perhaps have been expected if Chinese Marxists had followed the Russian pattern. The reasons for this may be that unlike other religions of foreign origin (notably Christianity) the adherents of Buddhism in China are numbered in millions, its international connections are with other *Asian* countries, and due to its long history in China it can fairly be said to have become almost an integral part of Chinese culture. For these reasons it was less likely than Roman Catholicism or Western Protestan-

[1] Op. cit., p. 160.

tism to present any serious hostility or opposition to Chinese Communist rule. Moreover, through its connections with other, non-aligned Asian countries (especially those of South-East Asia), Buddhism is a potentially useful adjunct to Chinese Communist foreign policy. Hence, the People's Republic has encouraged pilgrimages by Chinese Buddhists to other Buddhist countries and has facilitated the visits of foreign Buddhists to China. This is largely no doubt due to a desire to create the impression in the rest of Asia that a Communist régime, whatever its attitude may be to Western religion, is by no means hostile to Buddhism.

In China, however, this leniency towards Buddhism may undoubtedly to some extent be a re-expression of the old, basic attitude towards religion 'as natural to the common people, to be tolerated, humoured, even patronized, so long as it kept the people contented, obedient to their rulers, and faithful to the governing ethic of Confucian doctrine'.[1] Substitute the word 'Communist' for 'Confucian' in this statement, and it might very well apply to the present situation.

Another reason, however, why there may be less incompatibility between Marxism and Buddhism as it exists in Asia than between Marxism and Christianity as it existed in nineteenth-century Europe could be that in Russia the revolutionaries were confronted by the deeply entrenched institutionalism of the Orthodox Church and its apparent acquiescence in social injustices, whereas in China the revolutionaries inherited a somewhat different situation from that which Marx had known in Western Europe and Lenin had known in Russia. In China the religion of the masses, whether the ancient poly-theism, or a mixture of this with Taoism or Buddhism, or Buddhism in its purer forms, was in no case embodied in highly organized institutions. To some extent, of course,

[1] C. P. Fitzgerald, *The Chinese View of Their Place in the World* (1964), p. 31.

Buddhism in so far as it was monastic was institutionalized, but it had very little in the way of financial resources, or of vested interest in the nexus between Church and State, and there was, as C. K. Yang has written, 'no powerful centralized priesthood to dominate religious life or to direct operation of the secular social institutes.'[1]

The only parallel in China to the Russian religious situation was the presence of the Catholic Church, but this constituted only a small minority group, and its influence could be effectively countered by a Communist government on the grounds that it was foreign, Western, and a potential channel of espionage and subversion, rather than by any widespread attack on religion as such.

The institutional weakness of popular religion in China has been fastened on by some observers[2] as the *main* reason for the more lenient policy adopted by the Chinese revolutionaries, compared with that of the Russians.

We need to remind ourselves, however, that the Marxist criticism of religion is twofold: social and cognitive. The religion of the Russian Orthodox Church was opposed by Marxists on both grounds: social, in that it was associated with a social structure which represented a self-alienation within humanity;[3] and cognitive in that its practices manifested a quality of superstition which revealed an imperfect understanding of the universe and of man's place in it. Communism in China has apparently seen some need to press the second of these charges against religion, in its opposition to polytheistic

[1] C. K. Yang, *Religion in Chinese Society* (Berkeley and Los Angeles: University of California Press, 1961), p. 339.

[2] For example, by W. Lee, in the article, 'General Aspects of Chinese Communist Religious Policy, with Soviet Comparisons', *China Quarterly*, July–Sept. 1964, p. 161; and C. K. Yang, op. cit., p. 387.

[3] This point will be dealt with more fully in Ch. 9.

beliefs and practices, but less grounds, apparently, for bringing the first.

So far as Marxist hostility to the 'superstitious' element in religion is concerned this can hardly dismay the Buddhist. On cognitive grounds Buddhism is at one with Marxism in its criticism of superstition. The Buddhist Dharma represents no less radical a view of the universe; the difference between the two systems is that Buddhism has been content to wean men away from polytheistic and animistic ideas more gently and gradually, and has made use of such ideas in the construction of bridges by means of which the villagers of Asia could be brought to the place of Buddhist understanding, and see natural phenomena and physical and mental events from a Buddhist point of view.

If however men no longer need *these* bridges because they no longer start from an animistic or polytheistic position, then Buddhism can quite happily abandon them. This is not to say that they will not need *some* bridge or other, to help them in the transition from the everyday world of 'common sense' to the profounder viewpoint of Buddhism, but this is another matter. The Marxist rejection of ancient polytheistic ways of thought does not affect Buddhism in any fundamental sense.

There is one direction, however, in which the Chinese Communists might be thought to have revealed a basic attitude of direct hostility towards Buddhism, and that is in their action against Tibet. This is a matter about which European Buddhists and Buddhist sympathizers sometimes feel very strongly; because they do, and because they see themselves as champions of the cause of the Dalai Lama and his fellow-exiles, they sometimes take up an anti-Chinese Communist attitude, or even an anti-Chinese Buddhist attitude. Mr. Christmas Humphreys, for example, has described delegates from People's China to the congress of the World Fellowship of Buddhists as men who 'frankly care nothing whatsoever for Buddhism, save as it can be used to serve their own political creed'.[1]

In a reply to this criticism,[2] three monks of the Buddhist Association of China were at pains to point out the feudalistic nature of the Tibet of the Dalai Lama, ruled over by 'big aristocrats who had held the darkest and most barbarous feudalistic power for generations, big landlords who had cruelly exploited great numbers of serfs and refused to make the slightest reform'.[3] These may be the words of Chinese Buddhists who have learnt their Communist lessons well, men who are acceptable to the authorities as representatives of the official point of view. Because the intervention in Tibet was carried out by a Communist government the reasons given for doing so are couched in Communist terms. But to foreign observers this action against Tibet appeared as something essentially *Chinese*, rather than essentially Communist. H. E. Richardson, long resident in Tibet, and an authority on Tibetan history has traced the story of Chinese interest in that land of mountains from the time of the Manchu protectorate of the early eighteenth century onwards.[4]

The justification in *Marxist* terms for what was patently a *Chinese* action may not sound very convincing when it is remembered that while 'society in Tibet was divided strictly into upper and lower classes, nobles and ordinary men, by a clearly defined gradation in which everyone knew his proper place', and while 'by present-day standards such a system may

[1] *The Middle Way* (Journal of the Buddhist Society, London) (Feb. 1962), p. 174.

[2] Published in *World Buddhism* (Colombo, Mar. 1964), pp. 8–10.

[3] Op. cit., p. 8.

[4] *A Short History of Tibet* (New York, 1962) (published in England as *Tibet and its History*), ch. iii.

appear outdated', nevertheless, as H. E. Richardson has said, 'that does not necessarily mean that it was oppressive.'[1] The same writer goes on to say: 'Western travellers, from the earliest pioneers in the seventeenth century onwards, have described the Tibetans as easy-going, kindly, cheerful, and contented. It is impossible to reconcile the unanimity of that evidence with current allegations that the people were downtrodden, oppressed, and exploited; and it should be added that in thirteen centuries of recorded history, although there have sometimes been complaints and even insubordination against certain rapacious officials, there has been no instance of general agrarian discontent — let alone anything like a popular rising against the government. It must be concluded that the Tibetans accepted their long-established way of life and their social inequalities not merely with passivity but with active contentment.'[2]

It is important, therefore, to see recent events in Tibet for what they are: the expression of *Chinese* territorial claims, rather than an action inspired by motives primarily Marxist. Above all it is important to understand that this was not an attack by Marxists upon a Buddhist institution, *qua* Buddhist. That it may very easily appear so is due largely to the peculiar nature of Tibetan Buddhism, and its unusually (one might say abnormally) close involvement with the affairs of the State.[3] Tibetan Buddhism was, as Sir Charles Eliot pointed out, 'the most singular form of Buddhism in existence, and has long attracted attention in Europe on account of its connection with politics and its curious resemblance to the Roman Church in ritual as well as in statecraft.'[4]

We may therefore conclude this digression on the subject of

[1] Op. cit., p. 15.   [2] Op. cit., p. 27.
[3] On this point, see Ch. 11, pp. 152 ff.
[4] *Hinduism and Buddhism*, vol. iii, p. 345.

Tibet by saying that this was primarily a Chinese rather than a Communist action, and it was directed primarily against the Tibetan state rather than against Buddhism.

Western observers, sympathetic towards the old Tibet, see it as a weakness in Chinese Buddhism that its adherents can adopt so uncritical an attitude towards what seems to them to be very clearly a case of Chinese Communist territorial aggression. This, however, implies the assumption that Tibet was never fundamentally a part of China. This is a complicated and controversial issue, and not every Asian historian would support this assumption.[1]

So far as the internal affairs of China are concerned, those same monks deserve to be heard by the West when they affirm that 'in our new country we find not only that our religion has gained such respect that it never had before and that we ourselves have been enjoying our equal rights of citizenship that we never had before, but also that the spirit of "forgetting oneself for the benefit of others" as taught by the Buddha is being materialized and that a society of purity and harmony is in the making.'[2]

When Western travellers and observers register their opinions on the condition of Buddhism in China today, some are optimistic, and some are not. One says, 'No other religion is likely to take the place of Buddhism in China, and there is no reason to think that the aspirations which have prompted Chinese to follow the Buddhist course in the past will not continue to arise. . . . If Buddhism survives until China is freer and more prosperous, it will still have to settle with historical and natural science. Some of the Buddhist tradition would not survive this trial by science, but it is reasonable to hope that

[1] See, for example, the discussion of the subject in the recent essay by A. Lamb, *The China-India Border* (Chatham House Essays No. 2) (Oxford, 1965).
[2] Op. cit., p. 9.

everything true and valuable would remain.'[1] Another says, 'We are seeing, I believe, the last twilight of Chinese Buddhism as an organized religion. The dispersed fragments of its cults and beliefs are being systematically extirpated throughout the whole of society. The Communist war on "superstition" in the villages is unremitting, and one wonders how long the peasantry will cling to its Buddho–Taoist folk religion.'[2]

What emerges from these comments is that *something* of traditional Chinese Buddhism is likely to disappear, and that something is the element which is incompatible with life in an increasingly industrialized modern State. The 'folk-lore' element is one which Buddhism can exist either with or without, as circumstances require. Or, to put it more accurately, one can say that whatever is the folklore of the age and place in which Buddhism is found, in these terms it will express itself. There is a folklore of ancient India, evidence of which is found in the Pali canon; another which is similar but not quite the same in Burma; yet another in ancient China; and another will no doubt emerge in modern China.

Some of the more pessimistic views of the prospects of Buddhism in China seem to overlook the necessity for distinguishing between Buddhist doctrine, meditation and monastic discipline on the one hand, and local folklore elements on the other, with which Buddhism may be empirically associated. Hence there is a tendency to identify the prospects of Buddhism with those of the 'Buddho–Taoist folk religion'.

---

[1] R. H. Robinson, in *The Concise Encyclopaedia of Living Faiths* (ed. R. C. Zaehner (London, 1959), p. 344.

[2] Arthur F. Wright, *Buddhism in Chinese History* (Stanford University Press, 1959), p. 122. A similar judgement is made by Holmes Welch, in his article 'Buddhism under the Communists', in the *China Quarterly* (June 1961), p. 13.

Such views may also possibly reflect a too positivistic, rationalistic idea of religion, one which seriously underestimates religion's natural vitality and its ability to survive because of its important functional value in human society.[1]

[1] See Ch. 14, below, pp. 206 f., 216.

9

THE MARXIST CRITIQUE
OF RELIGION

THE ATTITUDE TO RELIGION IN
GERMAN MARXISM

'THE criticism of religion', wrote Marx in 1844, 'is the beginning of all criticism.' We must now consider the significance of these words for our subject, that is to say, must consider what is involved in the Marxist critique of religion, and how far it is valid as a criticism of Buddhism.

First it must be noted that 'religion' for Marx and Engels was very largely the religion which they knew at first hand, that of Western Europe in the middle of the nineteenth century. To some small extent their knowledge was implemented and their criticism strengthened by the kind of academic knowledge of religion in other cultures which was available at that time. An article on British rule in India, written by Marx in 1853, shows some slight acquaintance with Hinduism, especially its social aspects,[1] and is critical, in particular, both of the caste system and the Hindu's 'brutalizing worship of nature', exhibited in the fact that 'man, the sovereign of nature, fell down on his knees in adoration of Hanuman the monkey and Sabbala the

[1] K. Marx and F. Engels, *On Britain* (Foreign Languages Publishing House, Moscow, 1953), pp. 377–84.

cow'.[1] When Marx wrote these words the comparative study of religions was scarcely in its infancy. Some would say that it began with Max Müller, whose *Comparative Mythology* appeared in 1856.[2] Certainly very little was known in the West about Buddhism at the time when Marx began to write. What material there was consisted of editions and translations of Pali and Sanskrit which were just beginning to appear — Turnour's edition of the *Mahāvamsa* in 1837, Fausböll's edition and Latin translation of the *Dhammapada* in 1855. Not until 1881 was the Pali Text Society founded, and even events like these hardly indicate a widespread knowledge of Buddhism in mid-nineteenth-century Europe, even among the educated. And a knowledge of Buddhist texts is by no means the same thing as an appreciation of the nature and quality of Buddhist culture and religion, as it actually exists in Asia. Hence, in whatever early Marxists have to say on the subject of religion, it must be remembered that Buddhism is left out of account.

Nevertheless, it was not entirely European religion that Marx and Engels had in mind in what they wrote. Already Hegel, who died in 1831, had taught his students to think in terms of a long historical development in religion. The ten years following his death are regarded as the period of his maximum influence in Germany. This influence can be traced in particular in two writers whose views on religion contributed not a little to the early Marxist criticism of religion. The very word 'criticism' was a watchword of the radical Young Hegelian movement in the University of Berlin in the eighteen-thirties, which numbered Karl Marx and Friedrich Engels among its members. Another was Bruno Bauer, a lecturer in theology who developed the Hegelian idea of the advancement of human

[1] Op. cit., p. 384.
[2] This is the opinion of J. Wach, in *The Comparative Study of Religions* (1958).

knowledge by the 'progressive puncturing of illusions' to mean 'the evolution of critical consciousness via the progressive exposure of dogmas'.[1] The starting point was an attack on the idea of the distinction between God and man. Hegel himself had rejected this distinction, and had taught that the history of man is the history of God's own realizing of himself within the life of man. It was this idea which Ludwig Feuerbach and the Young Hegelians proceeded to reverse, and in its new form it appeared in Feuerbach's *Essence of Christianity*, published in 1841. Feuerbach held that belief in God was the result of man's tendency to abstract the finest qualities found in human nature and to project this artificially constructed perfection of being on to a realm outside the human sphere and call it God. What are in fact human qualities then appear as a divine power or powers to which man aspires, or to which he is subject. Man is obsessed by his own religious imaginings or dreams, because he is divided against himself or *alienated* from himself. His belief in a perfect being called God is the way man, i.e. religious man, compensates for this alienation. Religious man, devoting himself to the God who is the projection of his own dreams is thus living in a state of illusion.[2] But why, in the first place, does man engage in making such projections? Why does he *need* to pursue such illusions?

The argument was taken up from this point by Marx. This critique of religion is accepted by Marx, and is used as an important means of understanding the condition of contemporary society. For religion, thus understood, is the symptom of a disease. The disease is man's alienation from his true

[1] R. Tucker, *Philosophy and Myth in Karl Marx* (1961), p. 74.
[2] For a brief exposition of Feuerbach's ideas concerning religion, see H. B. Acton, *The Illusion of an Epoch* (London, 1955). See also *The Essence of Christianity* by Ludwig Feuerbach, translated by George Eliot, with an introduction by Karl Barth. (Harper Torchbooks, New York, 1957.)

nature. The real causes of this are to be found in the distortion
in the economic life of man, and the distortion which this
produces in human society generally. Starting from Feuerbach's
view of religion, Marx uses it to point to the need to deal with
the condition of society. Religion is the symptom of a condition
that needs to be dealt with primarily at the social level. The end
in view is 'the re-acquisition by man of his natural qualities, a
rehabilitation of himself as a social being liberated from
enslaving alienations'.[1]

Thus, according to the Marxian view, religion arises out of a
sickness of society, a sickness which consists of the alienation[2] of
man from his true nature : of this sickness religion is the symptom.

The sickness of society is what religion indicates. It is an
aspect of man's alienation from his true nature, and for this
reason it must be opposed. If the real roots of the disease lie in
the distorted economic life of man, then if this is attacked
presumably the symptom (i.e. religion) will disappear with the
disease. Marx himself wrote that 'the struggle against religion is
. . . indirectly a struggle against that world whose spiritual
aroma is religion'.[3] It would seem more appropriate to direct

[1] T. B. Bottomore, *Karl Marx: Selected Writings in Sociology and Social
Philosophy* (Penguin Books, 1963), p. 22.

[2] In keeping with the now general usage the word 'alienation' is used by the
present writer for what Marx referred to as '*Entfremdung*'. It has been pointed out
by Martin Milligan in his translation of the 1844 *Economic and Philosophical
Manuscripts* (Moscow, 1959) (pp. 11 f.) that 'estrangement' is the more accurate
rendering of *Entfremdung*. This word would have the additional advantage, since
it is used in current theological writing, of reminding us that it is a concept
which, in Hegel's use of it, certainly had theological overtones. But so much has
been written on the Marxian concept of *Entfremdung* that the word 'alienation'
now has a special meaning when it occurs in a Marxian context, and it is this
special meaning that is intended when it is used here.

[3] Marx–Engels, *Gesamtausgabe*, I/1/1, pp. 607 ff., quoted by Bottomore,
op. cit., p. 41.

the struggle against 'that world' itself, rather than against its 'aroma', and that in fact is what the Communist revolution is intended to be — a direct overthrow of the falsely structured society which, as an aspect of its sickness, produces religion. The struggle against religion would seem to be relatively unimportant in comparison with this. As Marx went on to say in the same passage: 'The abolition of religion, as the illusory happiness of men, is a demand for their real happiness. The call to abandon their illusions about their condition is a call to abandon a condition which requires illusions. . . . The *immediate task* (my italics) is to unmask human alienation in its secular form, now that it has been unmasked in its sacred form.'[1]

Meanwhile the Hegelian emphasis on the historical development of religion had received a considerable stimulus from the publication in 1859 of Darwin's *The Origin of Species*. Darwinian ideas are fairly evident in Max Müller's *Introduction to the Science of Religions*, published in 1870. It is therefore not surprising to find Engels, in 1877, writing about religion as follows: 'All religion, however, is nothing but the fantastic reflection in men's minds of those external forces which control their daily life, a reflection in which the terrestrial forces assume the form of supernatural forces. In the beginnings of history it was the forces of nature which were first so reflected and which in the course of further evolution underwent the most manifold and varied personifications among the various peoples. This early process has been traced back by comparative mythology, at least in the case of the Indo-European peoples, to its origin in the Indian Vedas, and in its further evolution it has been demonstrated in detail among the Indians, Persians, Greeks, Romans, Germans and, so far as material is available, also

---

[1] Bottomore, op. cit., pp. 41 f.

among the Celts, Lithuanians and Slavs.'[1] Engels then goes on
to affirm that besides the forces of nature the forces of society
also play their part at a later stage, and the tribal or national god is
the result, representing the mysterious dominating power which
is exerted upon the individual by the society to which he belongs. Finally, these tribal and national gods evolve into the idea
of 'one almighty god, who is but a reflection of the abstract
man'.[2]

It must be emphasized that Marx and Engels did not simply
criticize what they considered the archaic forms of religious
belief simply because those forms were archaic and outworn. It
was the false view of man which such religion embodied that
they were concerned to reject. They rejected the analysis of the
human situation in terms of God and man because they had, by
way of Feuerbach's notion of man alienated against *himself*,
arrived at an alternative and in their view, realistic analysis: the
true dualism, they held, was not between God and man,
but between the alienated elements within the life of mankind
itself.

It is important to emphasize also that there is no clear
dichotomy between the earlier, conceptual basis of Marxism,
laid down by Marx in the philosophical manuscripts, and the
later working out of these ideas in economic terms in the
Communist Manifesto and *Das Kapital*. Some have claimed that
there are two distinct Marxes, one the writer of the philosophical manuscripts of 1844, a proto-existentialist, or an expounder
of a religious philosophy of human alienation, and another,
unaccountably different Marx, who has left philosophy behind
and is simply a social engineer who, on the basis of an economic
analysis, advocates revolutionary economic change. Marxists

[1] *Anti-Dühring*, from *Marx–Engels on Religion* (Foreign Languages Publishing
House, Moscow), p. 147.

[2] Ibid., p. 148.

themselves reject this view, and it has recently been examined critically by Robert Tucker, in his *Philosophy and Myth in Karl Marx*.[1] We shall return to this subject later, when we compare the ways in which Buddhism and Marxism respectively deal with the question of the 'self'. Meanwhile we have to note the conclusion which Tucker reaches, a confirmation of the view of Marx's followers, that the doctrines of the *Manifesto* 'evolve directly out of the Marxism of the manuscripts of 1844', and that in the *Manifesto*, as in the earlier manuscripts, 'alienation remains his central theme.'[2]

Thus the position from which Marx criticizes religion in *Das Kapital* is essentially that of the 1844 manuscripts; there is in both types of writing the same concern for the overcoming of man's self-alienation. Religion, says Marx in *Das Kapital*, reflects the real world — that is, the world of economic realities.[3] The study of religion enables us to see what is going on in the real world, for religion is the shadow cast upon the wall by this real world. In nineteenth-century industrial Europe men were suffering many miseries and indignities. Religion accounts for the sufferings of men, said Marx in effect, on the grounds that man is not God, that is to say, that he is weak, imperfect and sinful, and that there is no escape from this situation so long as man is in this world. Only in another world will man be relieved of suffering. This religious explanation, says Marx, reflects the realities of a capitalist society. A society which treats men simply as producers of commodities for the benefit of their Lord and Master, the capitalist, projects its own nature in its religion. 'My Lord Capital',[4] a tyrant with an insatiable thirst for sacrifice, for the living blood of labour, is the real cause of men's sufferings, and the real dualism is

[1] Cambridge University Press, 1961.   [2] Op. cit., p. 176.

[3] *Das Capital*, Book I, quoted in *Marx–Engels on Religion*, p. 135.

[4] *Capital*, pp. 677, 708.

between proletariat and capitalist. Christianity, more especially in its Protestant version, is 'for such a society . . . the most fitting form of religion'.[1] That is to say, it projects most accurately in its religious beliefs the realities of the situation, with its dualism of God and man, its view of God, and its insistence that suffering man must acquiesce in the will of this omnipotent God.

It is certainly remarkable how much support for Marx's views the Calvinistic Christianity of that period, and earlier, provided. It is difficult not to think of Calvinistic man as *grovelling* before his Creator. Whatever may have been the psychological roots of Cranmer's continual breast-beating and whether, for instance, H. A. Williams[2] is right in attributing it to a tyrannical schoolmaster, the fact remains that Cranmer's God 'seems sometimes to be a merciless egocentric tyrant, incapable of love, and thus having to be manipulated or cajoled into receiving his children. It is one thing to make a straightforward confession of sin as is done in the Confiteor at the beginning of the Roman Mass. It is another thing altogether to harp continuously and at length upon our utter unworthiness to approach God, as is done in Cranmer's Communion Service'.[3] The same kind of utter self-abasement characterizes the Christian hymns of Marx's time and earlier. Worms are recognized as a familiar feature of the hymn-writing of Isaac Watts, and the jokes to which these creatures have given rise are the happiest way of dealing with this element of early nineteenth-century Christianity. Such references are not, however, confined to Watts,[4] and the conception of man's relation

---

[1] *Marx–Engels on Religion*, p. 135.

[2] 'Unchristian Liturgy', in *Theology* (Oct. 1958), pp. 401–4.

[3] 'Theology and Self Awareness', in *Soundings*, ed. A. R. Vidler.

[4] Cf., for example, F. W. Faber's line 'Have mercy on us worms of earth' (1849) and T. Oliver's 'He calls a worm his friend', from the hymn 'The God

to God which they represent is one which could afford good material for the Marxist case.

Another well-known and particularly significant example of Calvinist self-abasement before God is that of Augustus Toplady, a bitter opponent of John Wesley and the Methodist movement. It is very significant that in an article which he wrote in 1775, he introduced his hymn, *Rock of Ages cleft for me*, with a dissertation on the size of the National Debt. The vastness of this debt is depicted in various ways — by showing that it would take a man counting at the rate of 100 shillings per minute, precisely 98 years, 316 days, 14 hours and 40 minutes to count it all; or that it would require 20,968 carts, each carrying a ton of standard coinage, to carry it all; or by showing how far the shillings would stretch if laid side by side; or how many men would be needed to carry such a weight, and the length of such a procession. This leads to the assertion that the national debt can never be paid, since it would require more money than existed in the whole of Europe. From this he passes to the subject of man's spiritual debt to God, incurred in continual breaking of God's law. The sum of such a debt is calculated on the basis that a man breaks the divine law once a second throughout his life, and thus in a lifespan of eighty years will have committed 2,522,880,000 sins. How ever will a man pay off such a debt? It is with this question in his mind that man then turns to his divine creditor:

of Abraham praise', *c.* 1770, are referred to in *Songs of Praise Discussed*, by Percy Dearmer, pp. 116–17. B. L. Manning, in *The Hymns of Wesley and Watts* (1942), p. 129, notes that the 'elder hymn-writers delighted in worms', and quotes Doddridge also in this connection. While he admits that these writers overdid such references, he also disapproves of the 'Keating's powder: a sort of spiritual insect-killer' which has been applied to hymn collections by later editors. This is why such allusions to worms are considerably less known to modern Christians.

'Not the labours of my hands
Can fulfil Thy law's demands:
Could my zeal no respite know,
Could my tears for ever flow,
All for sin could not atone,
Thou must save, and Thou alone.'

When religion was expressed in these terms, it is under-
standable that Marx should claim that there was a connection
between the Christian idea of God and 'my Lord Capital' —
the figure of the capitalist, before whom the worker might well
confess that even 'the labours of my hands' can never give him
any rights as a human being, and to whom he can only suppli-
cate for such crumbs of comfort as the rich man may care to
brush from his table.

The connection between the two sets of ideas, the theological
doctrines of Calvinism and the economic realities of capitalism,
was sufficiently strong to attract the attention of others who
were not Marxists, most notably Max Weber. Concerning
Weber, who may be regarded as a pioneer of the modern
sociological study of religion, it has been said that he 'became a
sociologist in a long and intense dialogue with the ghost of
Karl Marx'.[1] That is to say, he did not dispute that there was,
as Marx had pointed out, a *connection* between Protestantism
(especially) and capitalism; it was over the nature of the
connection that he disagreed with Marx. For Weber held that
religious ideas played an independent role, having social and
economic effects, and were not the shadowy epiphenomena
that Marx held them to be. And however much the successors
of Weber may have modified his theories, either by over-
emphasizing the extent to which Calvinism is responsible for

[1] A. Salomon, 'German Sociology' in *Twentieth Century Sociology* (ed. G.
Gurvitch and W. E. Moore), quoted by T. B. Bottomore, op. cit., p. 58.

capitalism,[1] or by maintaining that only at several removes and when other conditions are satisfied does Calvinism result in capitalism,[2] both they and Weber on the one hand and Marx on the other indicate the closeness of the connection between Protestantism and capitalism, even though they offer different interpretations of the nature of the connection.

The essential difference is that, for Marx, the *religious* element in the situation, real though it might be in one sense as an indicator of the degree of man's self-alienation, is in another sense only the shadow on the wall. To deal effectively with the situation, and to put an end to the human condition of self-alienation, it is necessary to turn to the economic realities which are adumbrated by the shadow-play of religion.

This is emphasized also by Engels, and accepted and endorsed by Lenin, who quotes the argument set out by Engels in his *Anti-Dühring*. Engels regarded any *purely* rationalist attack on religion — such as that of Dühring — as short-sighted and stupid (although this did not mean that rationalistic criticism of religion would not have its proper place). For, as Lenin later commented, 'such a declaration of war would be the best means of reviving interest in religion, and in preventing it from dying out'. Engels' point was that 'only the mass working-class struggle, drawing the widest strata of the proletariat into all forms of conscious and revolutionary social *practice*, will free the oppressed masses really from the yoke of religion'.[3]

Lenin himself italicizes the word 'practice' in this passage, and this serves as a reminder that from the beginning the Marxist concern with religion was *practical*. Marx was describing a certain empirical situation, that of capitalist society as he knew

[1] Cf., for example, R. H. Tawney, *Religion and the Rise of Capitalism*.

[2] Cf., for example, D. C. McClelland, *The Achieving Society* (Princeton, 1961).

[3] V. I. Lenin, *Religion* (Lawrence, London, n.d.), pp. 16 f.

it, and the role of religion in that empirical situation. From what Marx wrote concerning religion in that situation his followers have derived what has become known as the Marxist theory or interpretation of religion. The question which needs to be raised, in particular in connection with Buddhism, is whether this Marxist interpretation has in fact the universal validity that is claimed for it by Marxists. No doubt it was cogent in nineteenth-century Protestant Europe, but one has to ask whether it has the same force in Buddhist Asia, for example. In fact, what is commonly called the Marxist critique of religion would be better described as a critique of nineteenth-century Christian theology, and of religion only in so far as it comes within the sphere of such theology.

We shall come back to this point later;[1] meanwhile we must complete this account of the Marxist attitude to religion by considering how relevant it was, not only in Western Europe, but also in Russia.

THE ATTITUDE TO RELIGION IN RUSSIAN COMMUNISM

The Russian Communist attitude to religion has its roots at least as much in what is Russian as in what is Communist. That is to say, it is an attitude which was already in existence in Russia before the Revolution; it is the rejection of religion as the Russian intelligentsia and liberals knew it, as it was represented by the Russian Orthodox Church. From the time of its introduction into Eastern Europe Christianity took the form of a virtual identification of religion and the State. 'All the religious and political concepts peculiar to Constantinople were transferred to the banks of the Dnieper, first and foremost the idea of a monarchy graced by God's particular blessing. The people

[1] See Ch. 13.

were henceforth taught the duty of humility and of obedience to
their rulers.'[1]

Three important characteristics of the Russian Church have
been pointed out by a modern historian:[2] first, it made use of the
Slav vernacular and was to that extent cut off from European
learning and culture, especially that which was expressed in
Greek and Latin; secondly 'it set greater store on piety than on
knowledge', so that it had 'a pronounced anti-intellectualist
colouring'; and thirdly 'it stood in much more intimate
contact with the State than did the Church in almost any
country of Western Europe'. With regard to this third point,
the same writer goes on to point out that this very intimate
relationship of Church and State had become so close by the
early sixteenth century that 'the Tsar had come to be considered
a semi-sacrosanct personality with unlimited power, the
earthly representative of God'.[3] It was thus that in Russia all
authority, political, economic, military and religious came to be
concentrated in the Tsar, who 'ruled by divine right and was
committed to maintain and defend the rights of Orthodoxy'.[4]

Officially, however, during the earlier period, before the time
of Peter the Great, the administration of the Church was in the
hands of the Patriarch of Moscow. But from 1721 onwards it
was governed by a Synod which replaced the Patriarch, and to
which a lay official was attached, called the *Ober-Procuror*,
described by Peter himself as the 'Tsar's eye' — for 'he was
there to see that the Synod did nothing displeasing to the
Sovereign'.[5]

---

[1] Henryk Paszkiewicz, *The Making of the Russian Nation* (London, 1963),
p. 214.

[2] Lionel Kochan, in his book, *The Making of Modern Russia* (London, 1962),
p. 17.

[3] Op. cit., p. 36.   [4] Ibid.

[5] Bernard Pares, *A History of Russia* (1947), p. 247.

The relation between the Church and the State from now on was clearly one in which the Church served the State. Bernard Pares comments that there 'thus began a secularization of the Church authority, which was to have fatal results later,' and adds that the fact 'that resistance was not more pronounced, that public opinion did not condemn Peter even more than it did, was due mainly to the deadness which was creeping over the Church itself'.[1]

By the early nineteenth century the Russian Church had become 'autocracy's political tool, obedient to lay authorities, and administered by the chief procurator of the Holy Synod'.[2] The procurator between 1836 and 1855 was a colonel of the guards, who 'treated ecclesiastical dignitaries as if they were cavalry subalterns, and used his position to make the Church an instrument for the unifying and nationalistic policies of the state'.[3] One of the characteristic forms which this policy took was the persecution of religious dissenters, such as the *bez-popovsty* sect (the priestless) who refused to pray for the Tsar and rejected the hierarchical organization of the Church. In spite of the State's control of Church affairs, however, the clergy, like many others in Russia at this time were extremely impoverished, often ignorant, little respected by the people and so subservient and sycophantic in their attitude to higher officials that some-times even the latter found it unbearable.[4]

In these circumstances it is not surprising that by the end of the nineteenth century religion, as represented by the Orthodox Church, was at a low ebb. 'There might still be an icon in every *izba*, but the parish priest was seldom a highly respected

[1] *A History of Russia*, p. 247.

[2] M. T. Florinsky, *Russia: A History and an Interpretation* (New York, 1959), vol. ii, p. 798.

[3] Florinsky, op. cit., p. 798 n.

[4] See Florinsky, op. cit., p. 737.

figure.'[1] Nevertheless, among the peasants a traditional, rather sentimental loyalty to the Church remained; this was not shared by the urban intellectual, to whom the religious attitude of the peasants was sometimes both shocking and embarrassing.[2] It is not surprising, moreover, in view of the condition of the Russian Church at this time, that among the intelligentsia 'atheism and materialism were regarded as marks of a progressive outlook'.[3] It is this attitude to religion which was inherited by Russian Communism, an attitude which combined very easily with that of Marx and Engels, but which nevertheless is as much Russian Communist as it is German Marxist. Lenin carefully distinguished between the West-European bourgeois rationalists' campaign against religion and that of the Marxists. The former saw and attacked the *cognitive* roots of religion; the latter saw and attacked these, but also, and more important, what they understood to be its *social* roots. In Russia, he said, this meant a struggle 'against every vestige of mediaevalism ... and every attempt to revive it or give it a different base'.[4]

It was this mediaevalism of the Orthodox Church which was regarded by the Russian Communists as the reason for the pitiable condition of Old Russia. The priests were regarded as being entirely on the side of feudal landowners and autocrats, and are described by Lenin in such phrases as 'serf-owners in surplices' and 'mortal enemies of the people who stultify the minds of the people'.[5]

The attitude of the Russian Communists to religion remains fairly consistent. At certain times the attitude has hardened, as in the very aggressive anti-God campaigns of the twenties and thirties. On the other hand, where the faithful members of the

---

[1] J. L. H. Keep, *The Rise of Social Democracy in Russia* (Oxford, 1963), p. 4.

[2] See Keep, op. cit., p. 269.

[3] N. Zernov, *Eastern Christendom* (London, 1961), p. 197.

[4] V. I. Lenin, op. cit., p. 25.   [5] Op. cit., p. 34.

Orthodox Church, even including priests, are prepared to co-operate in the building of a Socialist state, the tone of the Communist authorities becomes more conciliatory. In general, however, the attitude remains one which is summed up in the following words of a recent traveller in the U.S.S.R.:

In Leningrad I bought quite inexpensively a folder of reprints of Russian and Soviet paintings entitled 'ANTI-RELIGIOUS PICTURES'. They depict the various rôles which religion played in Russia before 1917: a well-fed monk refusing a crippled beggar a crust of bread from his laden tables; friars firing canon on the St. Petersburg mobs on Bloody Sunday, 1905; a battalion of the tsar's army in co-operation with local priests conscripting peasants into forced labor; a detail of the torture chambers used to convert heretics. But contempt was not merely directed at the material abuses of the *wealthy* Church. Religion worked its most potent spiritual damage among the faithful poor. In one painting a long-haired fanatic with cross and chains lures dozens of delirious worshippers on to a flaming pyre. In another a ragged peasant woman kneels and lights the icon lamp by the bed of her ailing husband. 'Poor ignorant wife,' read the explanatory paragraphs, 'she thinks there is a god which cares about her and her fate!' Religion in the hands of the clergy made money; in the hands of the peasants it bred docile ignorance and apathy. It is the memory of this pious submission that so infuriates the new Soviet generation.[1]

It was this attitude to religion, adopted first in connection with the Russian Orthodox Church, which came to be

[1] C. Geppert, *Soviet Religion: In Ourselves We Trust*; an address delivered in the First Unitarian Church of Rochester, New York, on 27 December 1964 (privately circulated).

directed against other religious groups, such as Muslims and Buddhists, who are to be found in the territories of the Soviet Union. It consists basically of an opposition to what Communists believe to be, first, the gross superstitions associated with theistic belief, and second, the social injustices which theistic belief encourages and perpetuates.

The possibility exists, however, that this kind of critique of the ignoble elements of religion may in itself be a religious attitude. We must therefore examine this possibility, and see how far it is possible to regard Marxist Communism as a new religion.

10

IS MARXIST COMMUNISM
A RELIGION?

MARXIST COMMUNISM — THE
TWENTIETH-CENTURY ISLAM?

IF Communism could justifiably be characterized as a religion, as some observers would maintain, this would mean that, in Asia as in Europe, there is a clash of religions, ancient and modern.[1] But if Communism is not a religion in any true sense the situation, in Asia at least, may be seen in a different light; where non-theistic religion is involved there may not necessarily be the same degree of hostility between it and Communism, and especially in the case of Buddhism and Communism. This could hold some important possibilities for any estimate of the future relationships and development of these two systems.

Students of political science might claim that Marxism, and the Communist movement which results from it, are properly to be regarded as political phenomena. According to this view Marxism is seen as a purely politico-economic ideology thrown up in the history of nineteenth-century Europe which happens to have a special appeal to, and to

[1] For an example of this point of view see Paul Tillich, *Dynamics of Faith*, pp. 122–5.

Buddha, Marx, and God

correspond well with the needs of, societies which are in the early stages of industrialization.[1] This is largely because Marxism, as an economic doctrine, is principally concerned with the industrializing of any given society, although it does not itself lead to the establishment of a Communist state, however powerful its ideological appeal may be, unless there are other specially favourable conditions, such as the breakdown of effective government in the country concerned. Such were the special circumstances which made possible the Communist seizure of power in Russia in 1917 and in China in 1949.

Against this view of Marxist Communism as purely political and economic it might be argued that it ignores (1) the extent to which Marxism is concerned not only with economic analysis but also with analysing, in religio–philosophical terms, the human condition of alienation and with providing a cure for it; and (2) the fact that the popular success of any religious idea or doctrine may well have to depend on the presence of favourable social and political circumstances. In particular, Islam provides what might be considered an interesting parallel. The similarities between Islam and Communism have been pointed out by sociologists and historians of the modern period, and since the closeness of the parallel has been made the ground for arguing that Communism, like Islam, is a religion, it demands consideration here.[2]

MUHAMMAD, MARX AND THE TRADITION OF ISRAEL

Like Muhammad, Marx was an heir to the tradition of Israel. It is noteworthy that both were, in varying degrees,

[1] See, for example, A. B. Ulam, *The Unfinished Revolution* (New York, 1960).

[2] On the parallel between Communism and Islam see, for example, J. Milton Yinger, *Religion, Society and the Individual* (New York, 1957), pp. 120 ff.;

influenced by Judaism. Muhammad regarded himself as in the true line of succession of the Hebrew prophets, such as Abraham, Moses and Jesus. According to the Qur'ān,[1] Muhammad was 'the seal of the prophets', that is, the last and the highest. In the earlier period of his activity at Mecca there was no consciousness of anything other than continuity with the Hebrew tradition; it was in the Medina period, when the Jews of Medina had rejected his claim to be a prophet, that Muhammad's attitude towards Judaism changed to one of hostility and criticism.

Marx too was indebted to the Jewish tradition. His father's name was Levi, before he changed it to Marx to conform with the German legislation of 1816 which confronted Jews with the choice of living in a Jewish ghetto or becoming nominal Christians.

Herschel Levi was himself the son of a rabbi. He was received into the Lutheran Church the year before the birth of his son Karl, and Isaiah Berlin points out the possible significance of this fact. He notes that the hostility of Karl Marx to everything connected with religion, and in particular with Judaism, may well be partly due to the peculiar and embarrassed situation in which such converts sometimes found themselves. Some escaped by becoming devout and even fanatical Christians, others by rebelling against all established religion.[2]

But Karl Marx's Jewish inheritance shows itself in more than this merely negative way. No doubt his criticism of religion, especially that of nineteenth-century Europe, had its more obvious, immediate, personal roots, but it is also an attitude

Barbara Ward, *Faith and Freedom* (London, 1954), pp. 168 ff.; and, for a longer treatment, Jules Monnerot, *Sociologie du Communisme* (1949) (Eng. trans., *Sociology of Communism*, London, 1953).

[1] 33.40.

[2] *Karl Marx: His Life and Environment* (3rd edn., London, 1963), p. 27.

which in a very positive sense is rooted in the long religious heritage of his Jewish forebears, and this was not to be shaken off in one generation.[1]

MUHAMMAD AND MARX AS PROPHETS

Again, like Muhammad, Marx was a prophet, it may be claimed. Inasmuch as the Hebrew tradition allows that there are false prophets as well as true, the point may safely be allowed; and it might be held that there is something of the true prophet in Marx. Like the Hebrew prophets and like Muhammad, he brought severe criticism to bear upon the ethnic religion of the area in which he lived. For just as Muhammad denounced the ancient polytheism of Arabia in order to establish a new truth in its place, so Marx took pains to expose the extent to which European religion had its roots in what he believed to be the deifying of the forces of nature and of society. Just as Muhammad criticized Jews and Christians for the aberrations and distortions of the truth which in his view their religion involved, so too Marx attacked Protestant Christianity for the self-alienation of humanity which it seemed to him to entail, that is, its distortion of the truth about man.

Both Muhammad and Marx may be considered as prophets in another sense. Muhammad's message was basically the proclamation of a coming day of judgement, a day to be ushered in by the Messiah. Eschatology is of the essence of Islamic belief. It is with this future day of judgement in mind that man is bidden to submit himself now to the sovereign will of God, and cease stubbornly and vainly resisting God's decrees. Similarly, according to Marx, there is a day of judgement to come, a day which will be ushered in by that which, in

[1] On this see, for example, Bertrand Russell, *A History of Western Philosophy* (London, 1946), p. 383.

Marxian thought, takes the place of the Messiah, the triumphant proletariat. It is because the Marxist is so sure of this
future judgement on Capitalism, so sure that history is on his
side, bringing ever nearer the great eschatological event and the
golden age which it will usher in, when the proletariat will be
completely triumphant and the State will wither away and
man's self-alienation will be at an end — it is because of all this
that Marxist doctrine may be thought to have something of the
quality of religious faith, especially when such belief is seen to
be expressed in the Communist's fervour for his cause, his
enormous potential for action and sacrifice, and his intolerance
of other views.

Certainly it was a faith of this kind which inspired Muslims,
especially in the early period, when, impelled by this new
power, they burst out of the confines of the Arabian peninsula
and spread their new religion through one country after
another, so that within a century of the prophet's death the
Islamic empire extended from Spain in the west to Afghanistan
and Sind in the east.

MUHAMMAD, MARX AND THE SOCIAL ORDER

A further point of resemblance between Muhammad and
Marx is that each was a critic of the order of society which
existed in his day and each was responsible for the inauguration
of a new type of social structure. In Muhammad's day, the
ancient tribal society of Arabia was disintegrating, or, rather,
was being disintegrated by the growth in the power of a wealthy
Arab merchant class. In the city of Mecca at the time of
Muhammad's birth 'the merchants were adjusting themselves
to the new situation brought about by the Persian occupation
of the Yemen, and were apparently profiting from it.'[1] This

[1] W. Montgomery Watt, *Muhammad, Prophet and Statesman* (1961), p. 7.

meant that tribal ties and kinship responsibilities were neglected; 'in a mad scramble for more wealth every man was looking after his own interests and disregarding the responsibilities formerly recognized.'[1] It was a situation in which the old bases of power and prestige in a nomadic tribal society — namely personal ability and leadership — were yielding to the kind of prestige which a man gained as the result of successful commercial activity. During the 'hidden years' of Muhammad's life — the first fifteen years of his marriage to Khadijah — it was upon such aspects of life in contemporary Mecca that he must have brooded in his periods of solitary meditation, until 'eventually what had been maturing in the inner depths was brought to light'.[2]

The result was the formation of a new community, the *Ummah*. D. S. Margoliouth began his discussion of the Islamic state by pointing out that 'although we are apt to think of Islam as a religion, it was probable that the Prophet thought of it rather as a nation'.[3] This does not mean that Muhammad was not concerned with what in modern thought are regarded as religious matters; only that nowadays we distinguish between religion and society, between the sacred and the secular, in a way that Muhammad did not. What he established was a new community in the life of which 'religion' and 'politics' were one and the same, so that some observers see Islam as a religion while others see it as a political system, and neither view is wholly wrong, and neither is wholly right. To paraphrase Margoliouth, Islam in the days of Muhammad was *both* a religion *and* a nation. The significance of this, in the comparison with Communism, will emerge most clearly when we have carried our examination of the two systems a little further.

Meanwhile certain other features of Marxism which seem to

[1] Ibid., p. 8. [2] W. Montgomery Watt, op. cit., p. 13.
[3] D. S. Margoliouth, *Mohammedanism* (London, 1911), p. 75.

characterize it as a religion must be noticed. Besides the strongly eschatological nature of its doctrine, the evangelistic fervour of its adherents, their readiness for sacrificial action, and their sense of being in possession of an absolute and exclusive truth, there are such features as the prestige and authority which attaches to the writings of Marx, Engels and Lenin, an authority like that of sacred scripture, so that all Communist policy and action has to be justified by reference to these sacred texts, just as in Islam all must be derived from the Qur'ān. Again, there is the veneration of the founders of Communism, especially as it developed after their deaths; there is the same extreme disapproval and condemnation of any views or policies which claim to be Marxian but are seen to be un-orthodox or heretical; there has been, during the early period of the growth of Communism the role of Moscow as the holy city, and the Politburo as the guardians of orthodoxy; there is the quality of a conversion experience that often attaches to becoming a Marxist. All these and more have frequently been remarked upon.

HISTORICAL DEVELOPMENT IN ISLAM AND COMMUNISM

What is of particular interest in connection with the present study, however, is the parallel between the historical develop-ment and expansion of Islam, and that of Communism.

In Islamic thought the world was divided territorially into two parts: *dar-ul-Islam*, the area that is surrendered (*Islam*) to Allah, and *dar-ul-harb*, the area that is yet at war and un-surrendered. It is instructive to compare with this the way that Marxism also regards the world as divided into two: the areas where the proletarian revolution has taken place and a Com-munist society is in process of being formed, and those areas where this has not yet happened. As Jules Monnerot pointed out, 'Communism takes the field both as a *secular religion* and as a *universal state*,' and in this respect is closely comparable with Islam. In its earliest period, during the Umayyad Caliphate (A.D. 656–750) Islam was in a real sense a universal state, in which allegiance was owed by all Muslims throughout the extent of the territory gained by Islam, to the Caliph in Damascus. It was not long however, before the universal authority of the Caliphs began to break down, especially in the more distant territories, as in Spain, where the Emir ruled from Cordova virtually in independence of Damascus. And even from the time when the Umayyad Caliphate was established there was a dissenting wing of Muslims who did not acknowledge the authority of the Caliph of Damascus, namely the Shi'a sect, who held that the true line of succession in the leadership of the Muslim community was with Ali, the prophet's son-in-law, and with his descendants. There were the Kharijites, too, who were opposed to Umayyad rule on the grounds that the true succession to Muhammad was to be found among those pious Muslims who had allied themselves with the prophet in the days of his early struggles and persecution; whereas, they said, the Umayyads were sons of those who in the early days had resisted the prophet, and were only recently attracted to Islam in the time of its political success. The Kharijites were severely critical of the very harsh worldly rule of the Umayyads; Islam had been betrayed, they felt, and so their battle-cry became 'Leadership to the best Muslim'. There is here a curious parallel with Communist history, in the matter of the succession to Lenin, and the Trotskyite criticism of Stalin's rule as 'the betrayal of the revolution'. Disagreement about the true line of succession in Islam continued; and although a great deal of the early passion has gone out of the quarrel now, Shi'ites and Sunnites are still unreconciled on this issue, just as the Bolsheviks and

Mensheviks similarly remain unreconciled (so long as we do not completely *identify* Trotskyite and Menshevik, but use the latter term to mean merely 'not a supporter of Lenin', just as by Bolshevik we mean 'supporter of Lenin'[1]).

There are thus, it must be admitted, impressive parallels between Islam and Communism, and some of these are of such a nature that one might reasonably suppose they pointed to the conclusion that Communism, like Islam, is a religion. But there are also some significant differences between the two.

ISLAM, COMMUNISM, AND RELIGIOUS PRACTICE

Islamic civilization is characterized by both unity and variety.[2] This, too, is true of Communism. It is when we consider what forms the basis of Islamic *unity* that we find the crucial difference between Islam and Communism. For what provides the common ground between Muslims in every part of the Islamic world, in North Africa or China, in Persia or Indonesia, in tropical Africa or Pakistan, are the characteristic religious *practices* of Islam. It might have been supposed that it was their creed which united Muslims everywhere, but in fact there are, in Islam as in other religions, certain differences among Muslims at this point, especially where the interpretation of belief is concerned; such differences over matters of belief have been one of the major causes of the sectarianism which has been so notable a feature of Islamic history. The basic Islamic belief, however, which unites all Muslims, is the simple confession, 'There is no god but Allah, and Muhammad is his apostle.' This confession, known as the *Shahada*, is uttered

[1] On this see J. Plamanatz, *German Marxism and Russian Communism*, pp. 281 ff.

[2] See the volume of essays on this subject edited by G. E. von Grunebaum, *Unity and Variety in Muslim Civilization*.

daily by all Muslims, and is the first of the five characteristic
Muslim practices which are the real basis of unity. The others
are the prayers, at five appointed times every day; alms-giving;
fasting, especially throughout the month of Ramadan; and
pilgrimage to Mecca, wherever possible, at least once in a lifetime. It is these religious practices which have fostered and
strengthened the sense of Muslim unity, in spite of the great
variety of geographical and cultural environment in which
Islam is now to be found. It is these which form the bare
essential, the minimum possible, that a man must be taught and
must observe, in order to be a Muslim. As a medieval Muslim
writer expressed it, teachers are to beware of trying to do too
much; they are 'enjoined not to thrust precious stones down
the throats of dogs . . . that is, to the mean, the ignoble, the
worthless, to shopkeepers and the low born they are to teach
nothing more than the mandates about prayer, fasting, alms-
giving and the pilgrimage to Mecca, along with some chapter
of the Qur'ān and some doctrines of the faith without which
their religion cannot be correct and valid prayers are not
possible'.[1]

It is precisely such a pattern of religious practice which
Islam shares with all the other major religions — however
much some of these may differ from Islam in other respects.
Perhaps the religious system which, in general, is farthest
removed from Islam in its origins, its history, its view of the
world and of man, is Theravada Buddhism. Yet each of these
five religious practices of Islam has a parallel in the Theravada,
where, again, they are central and important. The ritual, credal
confession in a brief simple form is what makes a man a
Theravadin Buddhist: 'I go for refuge to the Buddha, I go for
refuge to the Dharma, I go for refuge to the Sangha.' We have

[1] Zia-ud-din-Barni, quoted in *Sources of Indian Tradition*, ed. by W. T. de
Bary (New York, 1958), p. 517.

noticed the place which regular devotions hold in the life of the Theravadin, both monastic and lay. Alms-giving (*dana*), especially by the laity to the monks (but not exclusively), is essential to the Buddhist system, and as in Islam it is the giving of one's resources for the support and maintenance of the community. Fasting, too, we have noted, is a regular feature of the Theravada; daily, after the midday meal for monks, and quite often undertaken as an act of piety on sabbath days by the lay people. Finally pilgrimage to the great shrines of South-East Asia and India, such as the Shwe Dagon pagoda in Rangoon, the Temple of the Tooth in Ceylon, or Buddhgaya in India, is a thoroughly characteristic act of piety in the Theravada, and, as in Islam, may be undertaken as the great religious act of a lifetime.

Here then, on the one hand, in such religious practices, is the distinctive feature that links Islam with Buddhism (and of course with other religious traditions), and on the other hand distinguishes it from Communism, where the ritual or devotional element is notably lacking. The regular repetition of a simple confession of faith, prayer, voluntary alms-giving, fasting and pilgrimage — none of these is a characteristic feature of Communist life and discipline.

On the basis of a comparison between Islam and Communism we come therefore to this conclusion, that while there are indeed some very striking parallels in the origins and development of the two movements, there is also a very clear and decisive difference between them; moreover the area where this divergence occurs is precisely the area which Islam has in common with the other major religions. It is the area of ritual and devotion, an area of human activity where men acknowledge that which transcends the mundane and the temporal, where, by their actions, they affirm the reality, in some form or another, of the Holy.

It is for this reason therefore that one is bound to agree with the verdict of Walter Kolarz, when he said that Communism was superficially described as a religion, but only by those who understand neither Communism nor religion.[1]

MATERIALISM: IDEOLOGICAL VERSUS PRAGMATIC

To return therefore to the alternatives which were considered at the beginning of this chapter, we have now additional reasons in support of the view that the encounter between Buddhism and Communism in Asia is not a clash of religions. But to regard the situation thus does not mean denying that there is a clash of some sort: only that it is not primarily between rival religions. If, when this has been said, one is still aware of the antagonism and hostility that can and does exist, in varying degrees of severity, between these two ways of life, one must seek to explore further the nature of this antagonism, aware that it is an aspect of that widespread antagonism between secular materialism and religion which is found in different forms in many parts of the world today.

It is possible, however, to distinguish between different kinds of secular materialism. One kind is that which is tacitly accepted in much of the Western world today, and can be characterized as pragmatic and unideological. In its American form it is very well described by A. B. Ulam; the citizen of the United States, he says:

'if he views his society at all, probably sees there no irreconcilable conflicts, no "inherent contradictions", only concrete problems always susceptible to concrete solutions. Economic ills will respond to material progress, which is taken for granted; political and administrative shortcomings can

[1] W. Kolarz, *Communism and Colonialism*, p. 11.

148

always be remedied by legislation and administrative measures; even the major social problems, such as the racial one, will be solved by education, wise legislation and time. There are no ineluctable laws of history standing in the way of common-sense solutions which will eventually be accepted by a majority of reasonable men'.[1]

Communism, however, while it is secular in its world view, is the following out in action of an *ideology*, namely historical materialism, and it is this set of ideas about the historical processes of human society which provides the framework and the reference for specific policies and actions; in pursuit of this ideology Marxists may sometimes act in ways in which they would not act if they were following a purely pragmatic course. Broadly the difference between the two kinds of secularism would seem to be that the pragmatic kind is based on nothing more doctrinaire than the idea of the enlightened self-interest of many individuals, while Marxism, as a doctrine of society, is in this respect somewhat more akin to religion, in that it allows for actions and policies based upon considerations which transcend immediate concrete situations and the interests of the individual.

It is for this reason that Marxism may be found to hold a greater appeal than the avowedly non-religious pragmatism of the West to men of traditionally religious cultures, *if* for one reason or another those religious cultures are deficient at the very point where Marxism claims to have most to offer — an offering of a quasi-religious nature — in its doctrine of society.

Now this is not the case, for example, in most of India, where Hinduism has its own ancient, deeply rooted and still vigorous theory of society, and there Marxism has so far had comparatively little appeal. But in some Buddhist countries it

[1] A. B. Ulam, op. cit., p. 282.

may be precisely this that is the greatest need, especially if those countries are also undergoing industrialization, in however modest a degree — as we noted at the end of Chapter 7. This might suggest that there are certain possibilities of coexistence between Buddhism and Marxism; such a coexistence, that is to say, as will not involve the repudiation of religion.

11

BUDDHISM AND MARXISM:

POSSIBILITIES OF COEXISTENCE

BUDDHISM AND THE STATE

In South-East Asia the resistance which Buddhism has presented to Communist activity and influence has been due very largely, as we observed in Chapter 8, to the fact that Communism is associated in Buddhist minds with two unacceptable features: violence, and formal hostility to religion. With regard to the second of these we have seen some reasons for believing that in China Buddhism may find Communism somewhat more accommodating than in Soviet Russia towards religion. We have seen, too, that in terms of the structure of society which each envisages as the ideal there is less disagreement between Communism and the Buddhist countries of Asia than there is between Communism and the capitalist Christian countries of the West.

In order to be in a position to make some assessment of the prospects of coexistence between Buddhism and Marxism in Asia it is necessary at this point to consider very briefly the question of the relationship between Buddhism and the State, in the light of Buddhist history.

The relationship between Buddhism and secular authority

has been of roughly three kinds. First, there was the relationship which existed in the earliest times, which was one of radical distinction. In north-east India at the time of the Buddha, the older structure of society, that of tribal republics, was being broken down by the aggressive new monarchies which were arising.[1] In the conditions of social upheaval which this produced the Sangha existed *over against* the increasing individualism which characterized life in the new monarchies; it provided uprooted individuals with a continuing form of corporate life akin to that of the tribal republics which were now disappearing. In this situation the Sangha was an affirmation of the collective, social dimension of human life, as well as the embodiment and the transmitter of Buddhist ideas and values.

The second kind of relationship is that which emerged when the Indian emperor Ashoka became a Buddhist. For this meant that Buddhist ideals and practices now began to be fostered and propagated by the emperor himself, who became a member of the Sangha. This kind of pattern is to be seen again in the rule of such Buddhist kings as Ral-pa-can in Tibet in the ninth century, Anawrahta in Burma and Parakrama Bahu I in Ceylon in the eleventh century, and Cakri, or Rāma I in Thailand in the eighteenth century. Such kings saw their role as that of *protecting* the Buddhist religion, purifying its institutions and encouraging its faithful practice. The pattern here is one in which the Sangha, as before, is the essentially Buddhist form of society, but now it is set within the context of a secular or lay society ordered by the king in conformity with Buddhist ideals. This pattern broke down in Ceylon and Burma at the time of the European invasion of those countries and the overthrow of their Buddhist monarchs in the early modern period.

[1] On this, see further, pp. 169 ff., below.

In these cases there was a reversion to the earlier pattern, a relationship of radical distinction between Buddhism and the secular power, with the Sangha as the upholder and champion of Buddhist Dharma and religion, although now with the adherence and support of the majority of the lay people, subject as they were to foreign rulers. In Thailand the Buddhist-monarchical pattern continues.

The third type of relationship is one which existed in Tibet for 450 years, where an entire society was under the governance of one who was regarded as the embodiment of a Bodhisattva, or supernatural Buddhist saint, a personage known to the West as a Lama. This combination of secular and spiritual power, favoured by special circumstances in Tibet, came to an end in 1950, and there seems little likelihood at present of its reinstitution.

In China, Buddhism's relationship with the State has been largely of the first type, although there have been periods when an emperor or a dynasty has favoured and even encouraged Buddhism. In China it has been the Sangha which in general has constituted the essentially Buddhist feature of Chinese society, and has provided the continuity of teaching and practice. But the Sangha has there been somewhat more open-structured, and less clearly marked off from lay society; evidence of this may be seen, for example, in the existence of 'secular clergy' or monks who have not received monastic ordination. A distinction may also be made in terms of 'public' monasteries, and 'hereditary' temples or monastic centres. The former are those whose trusteeship is vested in the whole Sangha, and whose members are regularly ordained. The latter belong personally to the head of the monastery, and the ownership passes from master to pupil. They are somewhat more loosely Buddhist, and in general it is these which have been responsible for the criticisms which Westerners have levelled against Chinese Buddhist 'monks',[1] for their corruption and laziness.

In the light of these considerations it is possible to conceive of a certain measure of coexistence between Buddhism and the Marxist or quasi-Marxist state in Asia. This could take two forms. One is the pattern that might emerge in China. The other is the kind of relationship which already exists in Burma, in the synthesis of Buddhist and Marxist ideas and practices in the context of a form of State-Socialism fairly protective to Buddhism.

BUDDHISM AND COMMUNISM IN CHINA

So far as China is concerned two alternative possibilities can be contemplated. These alternatives depend on whether or not Communism is a religion, or at least, a really effective functional alternative to religion.

(i) Let us consider first the consequences which follow if Communism is not in any genuine sense a religious force, which is the view set out in this book in Chapter Ten. If this is is accepted, the consequences for the Buddhist–Communist encounter may well be those of the kind envisaged by C. K. Yang in his study entitled *Religion in Chinese Society*.[2]

Yang argues from the fact that religion in all societies is seen to have the important social function of integrating both society itself, and the individual personalities of its members. He poses the question: is Communism capable of performing this function? Can it, in China, take the place of the older religions? To do this, he points out, it would have to be capable of embodying in its beliefs and practices some kind of 'ultimate

[1] See H. Welch, 'The Chinese Sangha', in *Buddhist Annual* (Colombo, 1964).

[2] University of California Press, 1961.

concern' (here he shows himself a disciple of Tillich), which would be acknowledged as such both by society and by individuals, and which would be effective over a long period of time, and not merely for the first few years while enthusiasm for the new State runs high. The situation in China, as Yang sees it, is that the coming generation, while it may have a sense of economic and political fulfilment and achievement, 'will be anaemic in moral integrative values, which up to now have been conveyed by the awe and fascination of myths and cults.'[1] The consequence of this, he considers, may be that 'Communism's probable inability to cope with all social and personal crises that may arise in the future would compel the people, when subjected to extreme distress, to continue to reach beyond the finitude of empirical existence and rational thought for relief'.[2] In this case, he foresees a situation taking shape in which Communism would supply the socio-political doctrine, and some form of traditional Chinese religion would supply the moral integrative force through its mythic and cultic forms, at least for the mass of Chinese society, if not for the minority of politically orthodox Communist leaders. This is a relationship which if it is to exist at all between Communism and some form of religion can be most easily conceived where the religion concerned is Buddhism, because on the one hand its non-theistic character renders it less likely to come into conflict with Marxist doctrine, and on the other it agrees with Marxism in the kind of society which it envisages, that is, one that is not characterized by class divisions or individual affluence.

(ii) But even if, to take the other alternative, Communism is to be regarded as possessing sufficient of the characteristics of a religion to enable it to be at least a functional substitute for

---

[1] Op. cit., p. 403.   [2] Op. cit., p. 404.

religion, then in this case also certain possibilities emerge which are by no means without some interesting and important implications for the Communist–Buddhist encounter. If such is the case, it is Communism that will become the dominant religion of the Chinese people for any future period that is worth discussing — that is to say, it would provide a sufficiently satisfactory means, moral and metaphysical, for relating the life of the individual to some greater entity, in this case the life of society, a means that would transcend the more immediate satisfaction of *economic* needs, and would enable the individual to deal, in a way that had meaning for himself, with the larger crises and questionings of human existence. If Communism were to prove itself capable of performing this function in China it would for all practical purposes have become the religion of the majority of the Chinese people.

Now even if this were to happen, and some humanists in the West maintain that it could, there is no reason to suppose that this new form of religion, Chinese Communism, would remain static in form and nature. The history of culture-contacts elsewhere, and particularly the history of religions, provides ample evidence to support the view that a static condition would be unlikely. Islam in India offers a good illustration of the point. No two religions could be more unlike than Islam and the indigenous religion of the sub-continent of India. On the one hand a religion that is sternly monotheistic, in principle completely opposed to the least manifestation of polytheism or anything that might seem like idolatry; a religion that maintains that its holy book contains the sole source of divine revelation, and is therefore deeply suspicious of any form of mysticism; a religion that is universalist in scope, seeing as the ideal for all mankind the religious brotherhood of Islam where there is, in theory at least, no distinction of persons, where there are no priests, and no hierarchical structure.

In contrast to all this stands Hinduism, luxuriantly polytheistic, delighting in a profusion of gods, each represented by his or her own type of image, a religion that embraces a variety of ways by which it is claimed ultimate truth may be known, which in some of its forms transcends or even denies theistic belief, and in others affirms that God has had many incarnations and still incarnates himself wholly or partially, in modern times, for example, in such men as Gandhi and Ramakrishna. It is a religion very closely associated with a complex caste system, each caste and sub-caste having its own fixed place in the social structure, the barriers between castes being so great in some cases as to prevent any normal social encounter.

Yet Islam, strong as it was in its sense of being a supranational community, and having established itself as a new kind of civilization throughout the Arab world and the Middle East in the first two or three centuries of its existence, in the course of its history in Persia suffered considerable modifications in thought and practice, so that there developed a distinctively and recognizably Persian form of Islam. Then, even more remarkable, was the way in which, for all its pride of conquest, its contempt for idolators and its original avowed hostility to polytheism and mysticism, it underwent in India so thorough a process of Hinduization that it is difficult for historians now to agree in their assessment of the Muslim orthodoxy or otherwise of the religion practised and propounded by the great Mogul emperor Akbar. Nor was he an isolated example in the Islam of India of that time; so widespread was the extent of Hindu–Muslim syncretism that it was with great difficulty that the more puritan of his successors attempted to recover something of the original, pre-Indian nature of Islam.

The antipathies between Marxism and Chinese Buddhism are certainly no greater than those which existed originally between the clearly-defined, prophetic, religio-political system of Islam, and the profuse array of mythologies and cults that makes up Hinduism. In fact, the measure of agreement between Islam and Hinduism in their outlook on the world and the meaning which they give to human life could be said to be virtually nil; whereas there are, as we have seen, and shall have occasion to remark further, some not unimportant areas of agreement between Marxism and Buddhism.

Even supposing, therefore, that Communism became, in a real functional sense, the religion of China, it is not improbable that it might be a modified, Chinese and even partly *Buddhist* form of Communism that developed. That it will be a form modified in the direction of being more Chinese seems fairly clear. The attitude of Mao Tse-tung, even in 1939, was plainly that of a man who was conscious of being first and foremost Chinese, but one who was also an advocate of Communism because in his view China needed Communism. In 1939, when the Chinese Communist Party had established itself fairly firmly in the north-west province of Shensi, Mao Tse-tung in a speech expounding the nature of Chinese Communism said: 'It ... upholds the dignity and independence of the Chinese nation. It belongs to our own nation, and bears the stamp of our national characteristics.' He went on to point out that the Chinese had in modern times been too uncritical in what they absorbed from the West: 'we should never swallow anything whole, or absorb it uncritically. . . . Likewise, in applying Marxism to China, Chinese Communists must fully and properly unite its universal truth with the specific practice of the Chinese revolution, that is to say, the truth of Marxism must be integrated with the national characteristics and given a definite national form before it can be useful; it must not be applied subjectively as a mere formula. Formula-Marxists are only playing with Marxism and the Chinese revolution, and there is no place for them in the ranks of the Chinese revolution.'[1]

Events since then do not suggest that Mao has departed from the principle laid down in that speech, and therefore in any consideration of the nature of Chinese Communism full weight must be given to the word 'Chinese'. And if, as is the case in the south of China at least, the word 'Chinese' means also to some extent Buddhist, then the form which Communism takes even as a comprehensive 'religion' or substitute for religion, may well be influenced by the Buddhist element in Chinese life and culture.

(iii) On the whole, however, it seems more probable that in China, as elsewhere in Asia, Communism will not develop in such a way that it will ever fully perform the functions of religion. For in Asia, including China, the appeal of Communism, and its continuing justification, is practical rather than philosophical. As John Plamenatz has pointed out, where Asian peoples do turn to Communism it is primarily because of an awareness that they have 'nothing to lose, and perhaps, in the long run, much to gain, if they are driven painfully forward by the Communists rather than trodden underfoot by native landlords and European administrators and capitalists'.[2] It does not follow, as he points out, that the victory of Communism everywhere in Asia is inevitable, but wherever there are poverty-stricken masses and backward societies which require stupendous efforts and the utmost faith if they are to be lifted out of their squalor, very often this will seem to intelligent Asians to point to the practical necessity for a Communist reorganization of their society.

[1] Mao Tse-tung, 'On the New Democracy', published in *Chinese Culture* (1940); quoted in *Chinese Communism: Selected Documents*, ed. by D. N. Jacobs and H. H. Baerwald (New York, 1963), pp. 75 f.

[2] *German Marxism and Russian Communism* (1954), p. 340.

That is to say, in much of Asia, and particularly in China, Communism is attractive primarily as a practical economic policy, a bold and drastic method of social reconstruction, and therefore all the more attractive because so often the situation seems to demand bold measures and drastic action. This *practical* attraction of Communism is particularly true in the case of China. The traditional Chinese view of the inhabitants of the Western world is that they are barbarians. Nevertheless, these barbarians are acknowledged by the Chinese to have developed some useful techniques which might with advantage be introduced into China and adopted in order to strengthen Chinese culture and values. 'Chinese learning as the base, Western learning for use'[1] is the characteristic way of expressing this attitude. Among the techniques which it is acknowledged might with profit to China be borrowed from the West have been included in modern times political ideas and techniques of government: first, democracy (which failed to 'take' in China);[2] and then Communism. The way in which this too was regarded as capable of being adapted and even perfected by its use in a Chinese context we have already seen. In making such a claim in connection with Communism[3] the leaders of the Communist Party of China were, says Fitzgerald, restating the old Chinese view that 'China was the centre of civilization', and that 'the ruler of China was the expounder of orthodox doctrine'.[4] It would seem, certainly,

[1] See C. P. Fitzgerald, *The Chinese View of their Place in the World*, p. 71.

[2] Fitzgerald, op. cit., pp. 40–42.

[3] As for example in the speech of Lu Ting-yi, member of the Central Committee of the C.C.P., 25 June 1951, quoted by Fitzgerald, op. cit., p. 48.

[4] Fitzgerald, ibid., p. 49. Fitzgerald has somewhat overstated his case, however. J. Ch'en points out that he 'jumps from dynastic to communist China, ignoring completely the intervening period of humiliation and growing nationalism which was characterized by introspectiveness and self-examination'.

that due weight must be given to the Chinese element in Chinese Communism. China's present leaders have adopted Communism as a useful, practical political device. This does not mean, however, that they are necessarily committed to the whole of its original philosophical basis, should this conflict at any point with what is characteristically and fundamentally Chinese, as the words of Mao Tse-tung quoted above indicate. What is often not recognized in the West, moreover, is the extent to which a view of China as the standard of reference for civilization is still accepted in South-East and East Asian countries, where things Chinese — food, customs, dress, ideas, and art-forms — still enjoy the kind of cultural prestige that attached to whatever was French at certain periods of European history.

Since what is Chinese may reasonably be said to include not a little that is also Chinese–Buddhist, the inference would seem to follow that in China today Buddhism may well stand in a more advantageous position in relation to Communism than Christianity does in Russia. Moreover, the Chinese pattern is likely to be at least to some extent the model for other Asian countries following the Communist road to national re-organization. In most of South-East Asia these are also Buddhist countries, and so the cultural pattern that has been outlined here in connection with China might conceivably become the pattern for those countries also.

BUDDHISM AND STATE SOCIALISM IN BURMA

Nevertheless, there is an alternative pattern of relationship between Buddhism and Marxist ideas which is already to be

(Personal communication to the present writer.) See also the article by J. Ch'en: 'China's Conception of her Place in the World', in *The Political Quarterly*, vol. 35, no. 3 (July–Sept. 1964).

seen, perhaps as a potential prototype, in the emergent situation in Burma. General Ne Win's government implies, on the one hand, a rejection of democracy as having proved unworkable in the Union of Burma. The policy declaration of the Revolutionary Council declares this in so many words: 'parliamentary democracy has been tried and tested in furtherance of the aims of socialist development. But Burma's 'parliamentary democracy' has not only failed to serve our socialist development but also, due to its very defects, weaknesses and loopholes, its abuses and the absence of a mature public opinion, lost sight of and deviated from the socialist aims, until at last indications of its heading imperceptibly [*sic*] towards just the reverse have become apparent'.[1]

On the other hand, the Burmese régime represents an equally clear rejection of Communism, in so far as this means 'vulgar materialism' and conformity to the policies of any external authority. There has, however, been a considerable acceptance of Marxist ideas. This rejection of the two alternatives which seemed to face the Burmese people is fully in accordance with the Buddhist notion of the middle way between two extremes, a notion that is deeply rooted in the minds of Burma's national leaders.

In this case it was the middle way between democracy in the political realm and free enterprise in the economic realm on the one hand, and on the other a form of Communism that would mean foreign control of Burmese affairs. To many observers, however, the 'Burmese Way to Socialism' programme appears almost indistinguishable from Communism. What has happened since 1962 lends a good deal of strength to this view: the abolition of parliamentary democracy and the virtual substitution of a one-party system; the nationalization of banks,

[1] *The System of Correlation of Man and his Environment* (Rangoon, 1963), pp. 46 f.

commerce and schools, and the development of co-operative schemes of production in agriculture. The official philosophy of the Burma Socialist Programme Party published in 1962[1] makes frequent use of Marxist ideas; it is based on a pre-conceived philosophy of history and doctrine of man. But, as we have already noticed, there are some passages which some Communists would find embarrassing, notably the references to the 'one-sided notions of some so-called "leftists" ' with 'their dogmatic views of vulgar materialism',[2] and the emphasis, which runs through the document, on the twofold aim of the Burmese Socialist system, to plan for the physical and for the spiritual welfare of the people.[3] Yet in spite of these sentiments, there have been clashes between the revolutionary government and members of the Buddhist Sangha. It would be wrong, however, to assume from this that the Burmese government is in all but name Communist, and that its Marxism has left no room for Buddhism.

Two important aspects of Burmese state socialism have been pointed out by Western observers, and deserve to be kept prominently in view. One is the firm action of Ne Win's government against Burma's already existing Communist parties,[4] and particularly against the Peking-orientated 'White Flag' Communists, the more militant and 'underground' of Burma's two main Communist parties. An amnesty was announced in April 1963 to allow talks to take place between the government and the White Flag guerrillas. After the breakdown of these talks, in November of the same year the government arrested 700 Communists. The Moscow-orientated

[1] English translation, *The System of Correlation of Man and his Environment* (Rangoon, 1963).

[2] Op. cit., pp. 33 f.   [3] See, for example, op. cit., pp. 31–33.

[4] See Brian Crozier, 'The Communist struggle for power in Burma', in *The World Today* (March 1964).

party have avoided trouble with the government largely owing to their less violent policy. But as Brian Crozier comments, 'all Communist factions in Burma are, in the last analysis, pursuing identical goals that would deprive Burma of her independence.'[1] Here lies the key to the situation. Burmese socialism, under Ne Win, shows itself above all determined to be Burmese. The affinities of Ne Win's régime are not with the type of government that Burma knew in the British colonial period, nor is his rule that of a Communist leader seeking to do the bidding of Moscow or Peking: the real affinities are with the Burmese Kings of pre-British days. J. H. Badgley has pointed out that the primary goal of the régime is to enlarge to the maximum the power of the State, to 'create a single political community based on a Burman culture', a goal which, as he says, 'is very rational in the face of the gigantic population thrust from India, China, and Pakistan'.[2] The same writer has seen grounds for emphasizing the extent to which Ne Win's government has moved away from the colonial governmental tradition; he points out that what is taking place is 'the recreation of a new Burman dynasty'.[3] This was undoubtedly the *aim* of U Nu's régime also; he too sought to perform the role of the traditional Burmese leader, and to many of the people of Burma it seemed during the time of his leadership — and especially in connection with the Buddhist Council held in Rangoon — that this was, as E. M. Mendelson puts it 'the days of the kings come again'.[4] This being the case, it was inevitable that the matter of the relationship between the ruler and the Buddhist Sangha

[1] Op. cit., p. 112.

[2] John H. Badgley, 'Burma: the nexus of Socialism and two political traditions' (*Asian Survey*, Feb. 1963), pp. 94 f.

[3] *Asian Survey* (Jan. 1965), p. 55.

[4] 'Buddhism and the Burmese Establishment', in *Archives de Sociologie des Religions*, no. 17 (1964), p. 94.

should come up for re-examination and for some kind of restatement, both under U Nu, and under Ne Win. The traditional relationship could not simply be re-established as though nothing had happened. The seventy years of British rule which had elapsed between the last of the Burmese Kings and the achievement of independence in 1948 could not be set aside as though they had never been. The position of the Buddhist Sangha in Burma had changed during that period. Thus both U Nu and Ne Win were faced with a dilemma at this point. As E. M. Mendelson concludes, after a thorough analysis of the modern situation, in U Nu's time 'it was too late to go back to the early institutions of *Sangharāja* and his subordinates and in many ways too early to move towards any form of centralization. The Sangha may have lost its leadership, but it had not lost its strength and independence, based on the allegiance of the donors in thousands of villages and hundreds of towns'. On the other hand, the non-monastic intelligentsia, while they wanted the monks to retain their position of honour, and to serve as representatives of the best in Burmese culture, also knew instinctively that many of the new forms of education which had emerged since the days of the kings were in conflict with the old, traditional monastic education which was the basis of the old culture. 'Being responsible for their country's fate in spheres beside religion they could not tolerate outworn ideas and the maintenance of a social *status quo* preached by the monks, yet they could not find a way of keeping down the monks which would not eventually do damage to their reverence for them.'[1]

This helps to explain the difficulties which have surrounded the attempts of government and Sangha to work out a satis-factory relationship during the Ne Win régime — why, for example, when in April 1964 the government ordered the

[1] E. M. Mendelson, op. cit., pp. 94 f.

registration of all members of the Sangha, and required a pledge from them that they would refrain from all political activity, there were immediate protests from the monks, culminating in the self-immolation of one of their number, and the subsequent withdrawal of the government order.[1]

Difficult, and indeed, strained as the relations between the Revolutionary Council and the Buddhist Sangha have been, this should not be interpreted as meaning that Ne Win's régime is Communist and anti-Buddhist. It is better understood as primarily *Burman*, but Burman with a new dimension added, one which the old Burmese dynasty did not possess, namely, the modern doctrines of socialism which had been appropriated by the Burmese nationalist leaders during the latter part of the period of British rule. The new régime has been characterized as one that asks of its educated youth dedication in the service of their country in accordance with the principles of both the Buddha and Karl Marx.[2]

To some observers this may indicate simply the contemporary confusion of thought in Burma. It is worthwhile, therefore, to consider the extent of the common ground between the doctrines of Theravada Buddhism and those of Marxism, the more so because the case of Burma could conceivably be repeated elsewhere in South-East Asia.

Perhaps the least important element in this common ground between Marxism and Theravada Buddhism is the non-theistic attitude which is to be found in both — least important because it is a negative feature, and not a principle doctrine of the Theravada, although in a sense it is fundamental to Marxism. The Theravada is not greatly concerned with the existence or non-existence of God; in its more popular forms it accepts the notion of supernatural beings called *devas* (a Sanskrit word

[1] On this, see J. H. Badgley, *Asian Survey* (Jan. 1965), p. 57.
[2] J. H. Badgley, op. cit., p. 55.

cognate with the Latin *deus*) but in general it is content to leave on one side the question of a supreme god as being one of comparative unimportance.

A closer parallel between the two systems of thought is the view of the world which each of them implies. In the case of the Theravada the world is understood as a flux of phenomena; nothing abides, all is *anicca*, impermanence, the continual coming together of material and mental forces in temporary collocation, to be followed by their dissolution and dispersal into other equally transient forms. A French Buddhist scholar, Dr. André Migot, sees this as one of the most striking resemblances between Buddhist and Marxist ideas, and asks whether the words of Engels might not equally well have been those of the Buddha, when he speaks of 'the great fundamental idea according to which the world has to be understood, not as a complex of completed things, but a complex of processes . . .'.[1] Elsewhere Engels speaks of all life and self-consciousness existing in an eternal cycle, 'a cycle in which every finite mode of existence of matter . . . is equally transient, and where nothing is eternal but eternally changing . . .'.[2]

Again, as André Migot notes, one of the dominant ideas of Buddhism is that truth is not *contained* within dogmas, but is *discovered* in the course of a certain kind of activity, namely, the practice of meditation and devotion, performed in the context of the practice of morality. Karl Marx expressed something similar, says Migot, when, in his Theses on Feuerbach, he wrote: 'The criterion of all truth consists in its verification by means of practice. It is in practice that man has to find the truth.'[3]

---

[1] A. Migot, 'Le Bouddhisme en Chine', in *Présence du Bouddhisme* (Saigon, 1959), p. 714.

[2] F. Engels, *Dialectics of Nature* (Lawrence & Wishart, London, 1955), p. 54.

[3] Migot, ibid.

Another important parallel between the two can be seen in the way that the Buddha, like Marx, was the inaugurator of a social critique. He was opposed to the political and social alienation of man that was implied in the caste system and particularly in the dominance of the brahmins; in so far as he was positively opposed to the theistic beliefs of his time it was because he saw that they were a principle support of the brahminical system, and in this his attitude is very similar to that of Marx, whose criticism of theistic belief was an aspect of his critique of the human condition of alienation, as he observed it in Christian Europe.

Theravada Buddhism and Marxism alike embody both a critical analysis of the present human condition, and a way of changing it; both are concerned with the liberation of man from his present unhappy condition, a condition conceived in the Theravada as *dukkha*, existential suffering, and in Marxism as servitude and bondage. Both are particularly concerned, although in different ways, with the evil consequences of human egoism and greed.

In the case of Buddhism this concern is something common to most forms of Indian religion. The problem with which so much of Indian religious thought wrestles is that of the empirical self, the egoism of the individual, and it is this which is commonly identified as the root cause of man's wretchedness. It is from this that the various systems start; the differences between them consist to a large degree of the different kinds of solution which they severally propose. The solution offered in Buddhism may be said to have two aspects, psychological and social. Seen from one point of view Buddhism is a system of psychological analysis — the analysing of man's nature into its psychic components, pursued with a rigour and relentlessness that aim at the destruction of the very idea of an ego or self. The end of the process is that that the ego has been analysed out of existence.

Seen from another point of view, however, Buddhism is the restoring to man of a social existence which he is denied in profane, non-Buddhist society. A modern Indian Marxist has seized upon this as the characteristic mark of Buddhism and the explanation of its historical success and development. It was, he says, because the Buddha was 'an unconscious tool of history' that 'Buddhism, from its very inception was destined to become perhaps the biggest socio-religious movement in Indian history'.[1] Briefly the argument of this writer is that at the time of the Buddha the old tribal organization of life in North India was breaking down under the pressures exerted by the rise of the monarchical system. In the tribal life men had enjoyed a secure life, marked by equality of status and community of possession. 'The age of the Buddha was an age when as a result of the development of the forces of production, the northern regions of India were witnessing the rise of ruthless state-powers on the ruin of the tribal societies. Trade and war were creating unheard-of miseries in the lives of the peoples; the greed for private property knew no bounds.'[2] In these circumstances, the only possible solution, according to Chatto-padhyaya, was that which Buddhism supplied. He notes how appropriate the words of Marx are to this situation: 'Religious distress is at the same time the *expression* of real distress, and the *protest* against real distress. Religion is the sigh of the oppressed creature, the heart of a heartless world, just as it is the spirit of a spiritless situation. It is the opium of the people.'[3] Chatto-padhyaya then cites, from the early Buddhist songs, some illustrations of the distress which was being felt at the time, which he calls 'a few stray instances of the "sigh of the oppressed creatures, the heart of a heartless world" '. The great value of

[1] D. Chattopadhyaya, *Lokayata: A Study in Ancient Indian Materialism* (New Delhi, 1959), p. 466.

[2] Op. cit., p. 498.   [3] Marx–Engels, *On Religion*, p. 42.

Buddhism, in this situation, was that it 'fostered a sense of equality and *dhamma*[1] among a people cruelly deprived of these in their actual existence. This is borne out not merely by an analysis of the organizational principles of the *sanghas* but also by the very theoretical basis of early Buddhism'.[2]

In a similar way Marx, especially in the early philosophical writings was describing the means by which man's greed and selfishness, exhibited in bourgeois, capitalist society and encouraged and nourished by it, were to be overcome, and man's condition was to be transformed. According to Robert Tucker, 'Marx sees the Communist revolution as a revolution of self-change, and communism itself as a new state of the generic human self. . . . It is man's "regaining of self" (*Selbstgewinnung*), "the re-integration or return of man to himself, transcendance of human self-alienation." '[3] The master-theme of the Marxian philosophical analysis is that 'the enemy of human self-realization is egotistic need; the drive to own and possess things'.[4] In the future state of the world which Marx foresaw, true man was to emerge, purified from greed because released from the corruption of private property and individualism; he would be new man, because fully developed 'social' man.[5]

In all this there is sufficient affinity of thought and purpose to facilitate the coexistence of Buddhism and a Marxian type of state socialism. In so far as the kind of Buddhism which accords best with Marxist doctrine is the Theravada, rather than the more theistic, or quasi-theistic Mahayana, there may well be a tendency for Buddhism in China to accommodate

[1] Presumably Chattopadhyaya is here using *dhamma* in the sense of righteousness, or that which is right and true.

[2] Op. cit., p. 499. It goes without saying that for Chattopadhyaya, as a Marxist, the solution offered by the Buddhist religion was an *illusion*; but it was a very important illusion, and the best one available until Marxism arrived.

[3] *Philosophy and Myth in Karl Marx*, p. 151.

[4] Ibid., p. 158.   [5] See Tucker, op. cit., pp. 158–60.

itself to a Marxist régime by moving in the direction of the Theravada, and discarding some of its more polytheistic, popular embellishments.

Both in the case of China, and in the case of any Buddhist state socialism of the Burmese kind, there are two possible consequences which may follow from the co-existence which has been envisaged here.

On the one hand, there might be a positive contribution from the Buddhist side, in the direction of a toning down of the more violent tendencies of the Communist state, as Buddhism and Communism grow together in the Chinese context. The way in which Buddhism gradually affected the originally aggressive and warlike tribes of Tibet should serve as a reminder that this is not an impossibility. Another aspect of this positive contribution from the Buddhist side might be the strengthening of the view that moral values are real, and not merely relative or pragmatic. It is true that in Russian Communism the attitude has been, in the words of Lenin, that 'we deduce our morality from the fact and needs of the class struggle of the proletariat',[1] but this is not necessarily implied in Marxist philosophy. In the Russian case there was a reaction to 'a morality taken from outside human society', which, said Lenin, 'does not exist for us.'[2] But Marx's protest against the human condition of alienation suggests a view of the matter which is more akin to that of Feuerbach, for whom moral values such as love, justice, and goodness were real, but who rejected the illusion involved in attributing them to a being called God. As H. B. Acton points out, for Feuerbach it does not follow that goodness, justice, etc., are chimeras, because the existence of God is a chimera.[3] The Leninist view of morality as entirely pragmatic is due to reaction against a theological or revealed

[1] Lenin, *On Religion*, p. 56.
[2] Ibid.   [3] *The Illusion of an Epoch*, p. 122.

morality, and is not the only possible attitude for a Marxist.[1] A Chinese Marxist, possibly more receptive to Buddhist attitudes than a Russian would have been to Orthodox Christian attitudes, might conceivably view the matter differently. So far as this is likely to be the long-term effect of Buddhism upon Marxism in a situation of coexistence it needs to be taken into account in any assessment of Buddhism's role in the world today.

However, if Buddhism does make any such positive contributions, they will be communicated through those features of Buddhist life which are characteristically *religious*, rather than philosophical. That is to say, through the practices of devotion and meditation, and also through the honouring of the way of the Buddha in all the affairs of the common life. But it is important to recognize that both are essential — the devotional practices, and the practice of Buddhism in the common life.

On the other hand, a situation of coexistence might conceivably mean the gradual erosion of Buddhism by Marxism, especially in view of the similarities between them as systems of thought, or world views. This could only come about, however, as the result of Buddhists' neglect or disavowal of the characteristically *religious* elements in their way of life. For it is through the *practices* of Buddhism that its principles are preserved and safeguarded.

In either case, therefore, it is Buddhism *as a religion* that is important. Having made this point, we can for the moment leave the matter there.

[1] See, for example, the article by M. Milligan, in *Marxism Today* (Jan. 1965).

Part Four

THEOLOGY
AND
RELIGION

12

THE RELEVANCE OF THEOLOGY

THE CLAIMS OF CHRISTIAN THEOLOGY

So far in the course of this essay the concern has been with religion very largely in Buddhist terms and in a Buddhist context. What has been considered in the foregoing chapters, and especially the emphasis which has been laid upon religious *practice* is, however, not without its significance for Western theology. By this is meant both Christian and Jewish theology, and, to some extent, Islamic. Before we consider the ways in which our study may have relevance for theology, however, we must consider, though rather briefly, the special claims which Christian theology makes in connection with the religious life of man, and further, what might be described as a theological appraisal of certain aspects of Buddhism and Marxism.

It must be made clear that what is envisaged in this latter respect is not a thorough-going critique of Buddhism from the theological point of view, followed by a similar theological critique of Marxism. This would in any case be virtually impossible, for while the second of these two enterprizes has produced a fairly copious literature, the first has scarcely yet begun.[1] This may be, as D. Snellgrove has pointed out, partly because 'there is no framework that will bring Christianity and Buddhism into a relationship which is fair to both of them',[2] and partly because the difference between the two religions emerges at a very deep level, a 'level of doctrine and faith, where few minds can penetrate and still preserve clarity of intellectual insight'.[3]

What can be attempted, however, is the setting out of one particular and possibly important criticism that could be made by Christian and Jewish theologians, criticism of a feature which Buddhism and Marxism appear to have in common, namely, *the extent to which they both appear to expose human life to a process of depersonalization.*

TWO KINDS OF THEOLOGY

But first we have to establish what right theology has to engage in criticism of non-theological systems of thought and practice, whether religious or secular. A Christian, from a partisan point of view, might consider it proper to pass judgement on Buddhist thought, for instance. On the other hand, the Buddhist will quite justifiably demand to know what authority or reason the Christian has for preferring statements which he finds in his scriptures, such as 'I am the way, and the truth and the life; no one comes to the Father but by me',[4] to statements found in Buddhist scriptures. If this objection is taken seriously, as it deserves to be, dialogue between Christian and Buddhist

---

[1] See, however, H. de Lubac, *Aspects of Buddhism* (1954), and *La Rencontre du Bouddhisme et de l'Occident* (1952).

[2] D. Snellgrove, 'Buddhist Morality', in *The Springs of Morality*, ed. by J. M. Todd (1956), p. 239.

[3] Ibid., p. 244.

[4] John xiv. 6.

must proceed from some other starting-point or it will be nothing more than a shouting-match. There *is* another starting-point, and it involves making a distinction between what may be called 'first-order' and 'second-order' theology. The quoting of scriptural texts as a method of argument belongs to second-order theology; and this will be subjected to scrutiny and criticism after we have established what is meant by first-order theology.

Briefly, by this is meant the kind of theology which keeps close to its source in religious experience and practice. In this sense, theology is a certain mode of apprehension of truth. According to J. K. S. Reid this is a mode which is unique, 'an element that cannot be replaced from any other source.'[1] Again 'theology has to affirm the epistemological validity and effectiveness of its own proper mode of apprehension, *fiducia*, or faith'.[2] The claim is thus that there is a mode of apprehension of truth peculiar to theology, and distinct from other kinds of knowledge, although not unrelated to them. What follows is an attempt to state, in summary form, the grounds on which such first-order theology seems, to the present writer, to be based. It must be emphasized that the following paragraphs represent simply an attempt to convey what an historian of religion finds on looking into theology, and what appear to him to be the important and significant things certain theologians are concerned to say.

THE KNOWLEDGE OF GOD IN REVELATION

The subject matter of theology is God's revelation of himself to man. The knowledge of God with which theology deals is a knowledge which God discloses to men, not a knowledge

[1] *Theology and the University*, ed. by J. Coulson (1964), p. 144.
[2] Ibid., p. 142.

which men themselves have reached as the result of a process of reasoning. But how do men receive such knowledge? Let us, for the moment at least, say that initially it is mediated through special individuals, generally known as prophets. The prophet is one who at certain times has had an overwhelmingly strong awareness of the presence of a personal, transcendent reality, to whom as yet, may be, no name has been given. In the theological understanding of the matter, belief in God did not begin with men's possession of the name or concept 'God', which then had to be defined or filled out. Rather, this transcendent, holy, personal being first made himself known to men, men to whom he was until then unknown. The initiative did not come from man. Man did not make God in his own image. Here and there certain men received a new, dreadful, challenging kind of knowledge, the knowledge of God. The reception of such knowledge, the disclosure of himself to men by God, is revelation, and it is this that forms the subject matter of theology. Theology is the work of interpreting and understanding revelation.

To receive such revelation is not granted to all men; nor can it be commanded or controlled or striven for by men, even those to whom it may have come on some past occasion. No one can say why one man rather than another should have been the recipient of revelation. But it is entirely harmonious with the belief in the existence of God which such revelations inculcate and sustain that it should be so. The starting point of all theology is indicated in the classic description of revelation which is contained in the opening words of the Epistle to the Hebrews. 'In many and various ways God spoke of old to our fathers by the prophets.' And to these words Christian theology adds, 'but in these last days he has spoken to us by a Son, whom he appointed the heir of all things. . . .' This does not mean that revelation has now ceased, but that in the Christian view all revelation has Jesus Christ for its standard of reference and interpretation. The 'gospel' which St. Paul preached came to him, he says, by revelation: 'I did not receive it from man, nor was I taught it, but it came through a revelation of Jesus Christ.'[1] St. Paul is thus a *prophet* of the Christian period.

How reasonable is it to accept such a doctrine? Is it possible to validate this kind of knowledge with which theology deals, the knowledge of God granted by his own self-disclosure? Let a scientist answer this question. 'The argument consists in pointing to certain data, with an invitation to regard them as signs and interpret them. This may seem at first sight to be a form of argument foreign to science, but reflection will show that interpretation is in fact very familiar to scientists; we speak of "interpreting" experimental results in terms of theories, and the expression is correct, for we treat the observations as signs of objects — atoms, waves and so on — which we could not otherwise be aware of. Thus the argument offered in revealed truth is not only intellectually respectable, but has analogies with scientific argument; and there is nothing incompatible between rejecting authority in science and accepting it in fields where human enquiry alone cannot give us certainty'.[2]

Stated in these terms revelation might be thought not to differ greatly from artistic inspiration, or certain aspects of scientific research — especially the sudden and apparently intuitive insight which has sometimes characterized scientific discovery, even though this may have followed long reflection and hard thought. It is quite proper to apply the term revelation to these other ways of discovering truth. For instance, in those cases of scientific discovery of the kind which has just been mentioned

[1] Galatians i. 12.
[2] E. F. Caldin, 'A Scientist's Approach to Morality', in the symposium, *The Springs of Morality*, ed. by J. M. Todd (1956), p. 282.

there will almost certainly have been a great deal of preparatory effort, in the form of the collection of data and concentrated thought and reflection upon it. Even so, the actual discovery could not have been predicted, in any of these cases. There was no certainty that it would happen — until it did. It is for this reason that it then bore the character of revelation : some further aspect of truth, new and unpredictable, has broken into the process of human consciousness. But the unpredictability in such cases may be held to be only apparent. This can be stated in Buddhist terms. It is claimed for the analytical psychology of the Abhidhamma that here is a method of knowing the human mind and its processes which is so profound and exhaustive that it might be theoretically possible to predict with absolute certainty the future content of any individual human consciousness, given a sufficiently complete account of the present total 'karmic' situation of the individual consciousness concerned. The Buddhist would claim, therefore, that there is nothing in the mental processes of men that is really unpredictable. Similar deterministic views are not unknown in the West.

What then can be the significance, if any, of Karl Barth's words when he says of the revelation with which theology deals that, in contrast to all other kinds, 'it is not an immanent, this-worldly revelation, but comes from outside man and the cosmos', and is 'a transcendental revelation'?[1] In what sense can theological revelation be understood as coming from outside man and the cosmos? Certainly not in a spatial sense. The word 'outside' here means that the revelation comes in independence of the process of physical and psychological causality, if the latter is understood in a purely mechanistic sense. Revelation, in the theological sense, is the unsuspected and unforeseen entry into the processes of human consciousness of a wholly new element, a 'breaking in' from 'elsewhere', that

[1] *Against the Stream* (1945), p. 208.

is from outside the whole field of human consciousness in which every individual shares. Quite feasibly the claim might be made for scientific discovery that it is ultimately of this character. And Christian theology need not be concerned to contest such a claim, since truth is one and indivisible and can have but one 'source'. This is stated in theological language by Aquinas, when he says: 'Every truth without exception — and whoever may utter it — is from the Holy Ghost.'[1]

Wherein then does the revelation with which theology is concerned differ from other kinds of revelation of truth? The difference is to be seen in the nature of the prophetic experience: the prophet, in the experience of revelation, is made aware of the *personal* nature of the transcendent reality which has taken hold of him. So far as Christian theology is concerned the critical revelation of reality is seen in a Person, Jesus Christ. In every field of human knowledge one has to proceed from affirmations of some sort. It is from this affirmation, that transcendent reality is *personal*, that theology begins.

Ultimately then, theology rests on faith. As Austin Farrer has pointed out, he who attempts to think about revelation (and this is what theology is concerned to do), will first have to listen to 'a good deal of positive statement'. He adds that it is not for theologians to commend the faith 'otherwise than it commends itself, or to disguise difficulties which may serve to prompt philosophic reflection', adding very characteristically that 'we are not here to throw sand in anyone's eyes'.[2] In a somewhat different manner Karl Barth makes the same point when he declares that theology does not begin with the question whether God is knowable. God is knowable because he is known.[3] Men did not start out with the possibility in their

[1] *Summa Theologica*, Ia, IIae, cix, I ad I.
[2] *Faith and Logic*, ed. B. Mitchell (1957), p. 107.
[3] *Church Dogmatics*, II. 1, § 26, 1.

minds that a being called God might be knowable, and then find that he was. It is true, of course, that once the concept God is in use among men, there may be some who will project from their own minds the image of a being whom they then *call* God. But this is not the God of theology; this is not the God of Abraham, Isaac and Jacob.

At this point the following distinction may be drawn: where revelation (that is to say the disclosure of truth) occurs which is not characterized as the *self*-disclosure of personal Being, such revelation is non-theological, and constitutes material for study by the natural sciences, philosophy and so forth. Where revelation of the *personal* nature of transcendent being occurs, this is the concern of theology. Theology thus deals with the specifically personal aspect of ultimate reality, whereas other sciences deal with what appear to be the impersonal aspects. It is this apprehension of transcendent reality as personal which the theologian seeks to set side by side with other kinds of knowledge in the belief that, whatever may be the case with other kinds of knowledge, the knowledge of God given in revelation is necessary and indispensable to man.

Now we must turn for a moment to the question of what is sometimes called natural theology. We have in fact already dealt with the possibility of natural theology by implication. For by natural theology is meant, very broadly, the knowledge of God which men may have *apart from revelation*. It is assumed that through rational reflection upon nature and man, upon the cosmic order which is seen in the heavens, and the moral order which is seen in the workings of the human conscience, it is possible to arrive at a knowledge of God, and that this is the *prolegomena* for the knowledge of God which comes by revelation. But we have already in fact excluded this kind of knowledge of reality from the immediate concerns of theology; from what has been said it will be clear that this kind of knowledge belongs to the realm of philosophy. What theology is concerned to point out is that human reasoning can never by itself arrive at the stage where ultimate reality is known as *personal*, unless that reality itself takes the initiative and declares its personal nature, and shows itself to be personal. In this case, the knowledge which men would thus have would be due to the action of this reality, God himself, in disclosing himself, in other words, is *revealing* himself. The only God that natural theology can discover must be an impersonal being known as the Absolute, the First Cause, the Ground of Being, or some other such name. Knowledge of such a being is not what is meant by theological knowledge. For theology, as Barth has said, is concerned with him who 'is called God and Lord'. It is the knowledge of transcendent being as personal that characterizes theology, and such knowledge could only be the result of God's own self-disclosure. If the possibility of such knowledge is denied, theology has no right to exist as an independent discipline. In this understanding of theology, therefore, natural theology is a contradiction in terms. It must be made quite clear that we are not concerned either to affirm or to deny the validity of the knowledge which so-called natural theology claims to be able to convey, but to point out that this can only be knowledge of an impersonal Absolute, not of God. If this Absolute gives any indication of a personal character, we are in the presence of revelation, and it is no longer natural theology. If it does not, then that which is known in this way is not the proper subject of theology, but is the concern of philosophy or metaphysics.

But some one may sense a difficulty here. In so far as natural science, philosophy and theology are modes of apprehension of the truth, is not the object of all their several concerns ultimately one and the same reality? How can it be, then, that while natural science and philosophy find reality to be impersonal, theology affirms that it is personal? It looks as though there is some contradiction. For although I may momentarily mistake a person for an inanimate object, this is only a temporary mistake: if I see a man standing very still at some distance away I might possibly mistake him for a tree trunk, but I should sooner or later discover my mistake, especially if he were to address me. Yet natural science and philosophy on the one hand, and theology on the other persist in their disagreement about the nature of reality or truth — whether it is personal or not.

There is, however, another way of approaching this question. It may help us if we remember that sometimes a human being is seen as something less or other than a person, namely, whenever he is seen from the point of view of any one of the specialist sciences. The chemist may analyse the human individual into a few shillings' worth of chemicals; the surgeon may see him as a complex of muscles, blood, nerves, glands and so forth; the psycho-analyst may see him as a mental agent characterized by certain neuroses; and while each of these aspects of the man bears some relationship to his existence as a person, yet each taken by itself, or even all of them together, is an incomplete way of regarding him, apart from the man as he is — a living person, in his personal relationships.

The various kinds of knowledge of reality that are provided by the natural sciences, are all, in some measure, pictures of reality. And yet it is possible that reality is something more than or other than even the composite picture which results when all of them are put together — if they can be! Indeed, theology is concerned to affirm (not merely to suggest the possibility) that ultimate reality, the Absolute, the ground of Being, is *personal*. But have not theologians here fallen into the error of which they were accused by Feuerbach — of making a god in their own image, by preceding in this way from a human example to a divine analogy? The theologian would reply that he did not initiate the whole theological enterprise by his analogy. Theology began when men first started to reflect and to reason on the nature of God's self-disclosure through the prophet. The God of whom men thus became aware was not one whose description they could have fabricated, nor was he by any means a projection of their own nature. One of the most usual features of revelation is the disturbing or unwelcome or challenging new insight which it brings. Characteristic of the experience of the Hebrew prophets is the reluctance or inadequacy which the prophet feels in face of the burden which is laid upon him of declaring to his contemporaries the revelation he has received. Equally characteristic is the scorn, or abuse, or worse, with which men often treat the prophet when he does so. Elijah fleeing for his life, Amos being hounded out of Israel because his message was intolerable, Jeremiah languishing in a dungeon, these are the common experiences of the prophets when they declare the revelation of God that has come to them. The theologian has to ask Feuerbach and his followers, Why does prophet after prophet so *reluctantly* declare the revelation of a god he has fabricated?

This then is the subject matter of first-order theology, the nature of God's self-disclosure to man. The method of theology is not to proceed from the unknown and by enquiry to reach some knowledge which is called the knowledge of God; but rather to seek to explicate and make clearer what is *given*, that is, that which has been disclosed in revelation. Finally, of course, theology rests on faith, but so in a sense does every other kind of knowledge. The sceptic, or the atheist, or the materialist, must himself either accept or reject the nature and method of theology, but before he rejects it, it is important that he should understand what it is he is rejecting. And this is very often not the case.

What has been said about the place of theology in relation to other forms of human knowledge may therefore be summarized as follows. All human knowledge may in some sense be 'revealed'; this is true of the kind of knowledge with which theology deals; the distinctness of theology is that it is concerned with personality, both in its assertion that the ultimately real is to be characterized as personal, and also that the *summum bonum* of human existence is advancement into such personal being; the means whereby this can happen is also the concern of theology and is usually more or less formalized as a doctrine of salvation.

THE NATURE OF PERSONAL BEING

This concern of theology with ultimate being as personal is sometimes misunderstood. The reason for this is that the word 'personality' is used in a number of different senses. One of these is the sense which confuses personality with individuality. F. R. Tennant pointed out that 'even theistic writers have sometimes evinced reluctance to speak of God as a Person. In some cases this is due to a leaning towards monism; in others to the adoption of a particular interpretation of the doctrine of the Trinity; but most commonly perhaps, to the belief that to ascribe personality to God involves difficulties suggested by our knowledge concerning the conditions of human acquisition of the labile status of personality'.[1]

This serves as a useful reminder of that use of the word personality which must be distinguished from the sense it has been given above in connection with theological knowledge. In psychology the word is used to refer to a particular pattern of psychological structure, or, more precisely, of behaviour, which may distinguish from one individual to another. For this reason

[1] *Philosophical Theology* (1930), vol. ii, p. 167.

in theological contexts it is better with John Macmurray to say 'the personal' even when it might seem easier to use the word 'personality'. For in theology what is meant by this word is not the set of characteristics which distinguishes one individual from another, but rather that quality 'in virtue of which a person *is* a person; a property therefore which all persons share, and which distinguishes a person from all beings that are not personal'.[1]

Another way of expressing this is found in Karl Barth when he declares that from the point of view of Christian theology it is incorrect to speak of 'personalizing' in reference to God's being, for this is to argue in a circle. It is human nature which has to receive the concept of the personal. 'The real person is not man but God. It is not God who is a person by extension, but we.'[2]

Essentially the same idea was expressed by Clement Webb, when he wrote, 'Personality is not merely something we observe in men; rather it is something which, though suggested to us by what we find in men, we perceive to be only imperfectly realized in them; and this can only be because we are somehow aware of a perfection or ideal with which we contrast what we find in men as falling short of it.'[3] It is from this point of view that the Christian theological doctrine of man is best understood: that personality, or perhaps better, 'personhood', is a quality of being rarely present in any full and stable sense among human beings, but is ever at the mercy of irrational and anti-personal forces which can at the human level diminish or even destroy this *personal* quality of being. This is the theological view of the human condition.

But in so far as human life does ever display this high quality of being which we have called personhood this in itself is a

---

[1] J. Macmurray, *Persons in Relation* (1961), p. 25.
[2] *Church Dogmatics*, II. 1, pp. 271 f.   [3] *God and Personality* (1918), p. 21.

strong argument for the personal nature of the Absolute. As Karl Heim has put it, 'an I cannot be generated by an It.'[1] That is, if creatures possess, even though often imperfectly, something of the quality of personal being, then this personal quality must be in the Power which produces the world and man.

Thus the question with which theology deals is not, Does God exist? If, as Macmurray points out, this presupposes an idea called God arising 'independently' of a knowledge of this existence' about which one then enquires 'whether this idea refers to any existent object'. (This is why, as Macmurray emphasizes, 'the God of the traditional proofs is not the God of religion.'[2]) This improper question, Does God exist? has to be re-expressed in the form, 'Is what exists personal?'[3] It is with this question that theology is primarily concerned, and to which it claims that an answer can be given. Notice, it is not theology that is able to give the answer; the answer is given in the life of religion, in religious encounter, in the experience of outstanding human beings. Theology depends on this, and issues from it; it is in this sense akin to poetry, if this can be regarded as 'emotion recollected in tranquility'. Only, theology would claim more for the primary experience; as consisting not only of emotion, but also of the deepest kind of *knowledge*.

It is this emphasis on the cruciality of the personal that is characteristic of a great deal of modern theological thought, indeed, one is compelled to say, of the most *vital* and relevant theological thought. The names of F. R. Tennant, Clement Webb, Karl Heim, and John Macmurray have already been mentioned. One could add, especially, those of Martin Buber, Nicholas Berdyaev and Jacques Maritain.

Here, then, is the relevance of theology in association with other forms of human knowledge: the theological understand-

[1] *Christian Faith and Natural Science* (1953), pp. 208 ff.
[2] *Persons in Relation*, p. 207.   [3] See op. cit., pp. 215–19.

ing of man's existence is something which demands to be taken seriously. So long as theology keeps close to the source of its own special insight it remains vital and important; it makes an affirmation about the human condition which demands at least as serious consideration as the kind of affirmations about human nature made by natural science, social science, and the arts. Indeed, in making its own characteristic affirmation theology corroborates what is even partially and perhaps obscurely perceived in these other forms of human knowledge: namely, that it is in moving towards *fully personal being* that human nature finds its own meaning and ultimate purpose. Thus, for example, in a discussion of the apparent conflict between faith and reason, Michael Polanyi[1] writes: 'The kind of knowledge which I am vindicating here, and which I call *personal knowledge*, casts aside these absurdities of the current scientific approach and reconciles the process of knowing with the acts of addressing another person. In doing so, it establishes a continuous ascent from our less personal knowing of inanimate matter to our convivial knowing of living beings and beyond this to the knowing of our responsible fellow men. Such I believe is the true transition from the science to the humanities and also from our knowing the person of God.'[2]

PERSONAL AND ANTI-PERSONAL IN MARXISM AND BUDDHISM

This kind of affirmation is certainly no irrelevance in the modern world. Anyone, whether as scientist, artist, or theologian, who seeks to vindicate the value of personal being is involved in a situation of conflict — conflict with political and technological forces present in the modern situations which everywhere militate against the personal.

[1] In *The Journal of Religion* (Chicago, Oct. 1961).   [2] Ibid., p. 245.

In the actual course of its history, in Russia at least, Communism appears to have been one such force. This is an effect which seems to be directly contrary to Marx's original concern. The new 'social man' of Marx's vision, freed from the alienation and corruption of private property and individualism, might have been a more truly personal being, in so far as he *was* free from isolating individualism and able to enter more fully into a wider life of social relationships. But in fact what Communist totalitarianism appears to have done is merely to 'socialize' the human individual out of existence in the interests of the omnicompetent State without any such development in the direction of personal being as might have been hoped for or expected by Marx. Instead it has resulted in what Berdyaev has characterized as the 'inhumanity' of Communism,[1] and which in Berdyaev's view is something dark and demoniacal. It is, he says, this positively demoniacal element that gives it its dynamism, and can be seen in the characteristic method of Marxist Communism, the canalizing and directing of feelings of resentment, envy, hatred and revenge.

It is this in Communism which theology, from its own position of affirming the supreme value of the personal, believes it has the right and the duty to criticize and to resist.

What of the theological critique of the devaluation of personal being in Buddhism? For something of the same kind that happens in Communism might be expected to happen in Buddhism, namely, the devaluation of personal being — only here it would be not because the individual has been destroyed by being *socialized* out of existence, but rather, *conceptually analysed* out of existence. As we noted in the previous chapter, there is a close parallel at this point between Buddhism and Marxism, in the way in which Buddhism also is concerned with the problem of the egocentric individual, and the need for

[1] *The Russian Revolution* (1933), pp. 84 f.

making known and available to men a new, supra-individual sphere of existence. Might there not be a danger that what happens in Communism happens in Buddhism also, that individualism is dissolved without real personal existence being brought any nearer?

It must be admitted that if Buddhism were to find itself in a situation of tolerable coexistence with Marxism there might be a danger of this kind. Because of its analytical denial of any permanent self or ego, Buddhism might be thought to be particularly vulnerable to the Communist violation of the personal. Conceptually, it might be argued, Buddhism is wide open to the Communist kind of collectivism. However, as we have already seen, at the devotional and religious-practical level Buddhism can prove resistant to Communism; all the greater importance would therefore attach, in such a situation, to the checks and balances which devotion and religious practice provide to the dangers which may possibly exist at the conceptual level.

Where Buddhism exists in a less dangerous context, that is, where it is not subject to the positively depersonalizing effect of Communism it has its own sufficient reasons for not running out into a bleak depersonalizing of human life.

This may sound surprising, especially to those in the West whose understanding of Buddhism is limited to its *analytical* aspect, that is to say, who are familiar with the idea that Buddhist thought resolves the individual into a flux of elements, mental and physical, having no permanent significance. This is a true account of Buddhist thought so far as it goes, but it does not go far enough. Beyond the analytical method employed in Buddhist philosophy there is another, the relational. It is important to remember that these two methods are complementary. The entire body of literature known as the Abhidhamma has this twofold process as its basis. While one of the principal books of the Abhidhamma is concerned with rigorous analysis[1] (such as that of the individual 'self' into its constitutive 'parts', themselves also subject to further analysis, and so on) another book[2] deals with the 'vast net of relational categories'[3] in the context of which such factors exist, and with the possibilities of recombining such factors in new patterns. In yet another work of the Abhidhamma[4] both methods, the analytical and the synthetical, are exemplified and harmonized at the same time'.[5]

Enough has been said at least to indicate that Buddhist thought is not merely analytical. Indeed, without its relational method, and the recombining of the constituent factors into new and more wholesome patterns, Buddhism would be deprived of its essential nature.

So far as the analysis of the individual is concerned, it may be said, briefly and summarily, that the intention in Buddhism is that the mental and physical or 'karmic' events into which the so-called isolated self may be resolved are to be related to other 'events' in such a way that a new and better combination will result. This process is to be continued patiently, through long periods of time and many 'individual existences', until the ultimate is reached, which is nothing less than that level of being which is best described as the Buddha-nature.

This aspiration away from egocentric individualism towards the Buddha-nature involves the continual refashioning and refining of relationships with other beings of every kind, a process which may in fact be said to be of a very similar nature to that envisaged in the theological account of human existence, the constant growing into true personal being. There is need for very much more exploration of the common ground which

[1] *Dhammasangani.*   [2] *Patthāna.*
[3] Nyanaponika Mahathera, *Abhidhamma Studies* (Colombo, 1949), p. 3.
[4] *Vibhanga.*   [5] Nyanaponika, op. cit., p. 5.

exists here between Buddhist and Christian thought than has yet been attempted.

In Buddhism the end is kept steadily in view, and the disciple of the Buddha is kept safely in the path of spiritual progress towards this end, by loyal and regular adherence to the discipline of ritual devotion and meditation. Where this happens there is a genuine heightening of personal being and a quiet, calm saintliness that is unmistakable. But where the religious discipline is neglected, there is found that rank growth of bigotry and hypocrisy which, as we noted earlier, is a slur upon the name of Buddhism.[1]

Buddhism, however, is not alone in this. The theological tradition of the West has not everywhere resulted in a growth towards true personal being. Why this is so we must now consider.

---

[1] See also below, p. 214

13

IRRELEVANT THEOLOGY

FEUERBACH VINDICATED

BOTH in view of what was said at the end of the last chapter, and of the conclusion reached in Chapter Nine,[1] that the Marxist critique of 'religion' is really a critique of nineteenth-century Western theology, we must now consider more closely the kind of judgement on theology which has been implied in this study. That is to say we must consider how far the strictures of Feuerbach and Marx on theology were, *and still are*, justified; and also how far this is due to the weakening within *Western* Christianity of those elements of religious life and practice which have been preserved elsewhere, both in Christianity and in Buddhism.

A great deal of the intellectual activity that goes by the name of theology does not justify J. K. S. Reid's claim that theology is a 'mode of apprehension of truth'. Far from this, a great deal of contemporary theology consists of the continual analysis and re-analysis, the sifting and sorting and discussing (nowadays possibly even with the aid of computers!) of what was first apprehended long ago in prophetic and mystical experience.

[1] See above, p. 130 f.

The primary expression of that encounter which the prophetic-mystic had with the personal at a transcendental level is what we have described as first-order or mystical theology, and this consists wholly of the attempt by those who had entered into the experience to convey the nature of their encounter with the personal-holy, attempts which inevitably have to employ parable and allegory. A great part of the writings which make up the New Testament are of this character, and need to be interpreted from this understanding, instead of being regarded as though they were of the same order as legal codes or even railway timetables which needed but to be deciphered by an intelligent clerk. Rather the affinity is with other literary art-forms, poetic and symbolic.[1]

It is for this reason that literary criticism has much more significance for theology than has been yet sufficiently acknowledged in the 'biblical theology' of the modern period. The close connection between prophecy and poetry goes deeper than the kind of view of poetry common in theological circles would allow. Poetry is not merely a different, possibly more elegant way of saying things than prose. As E. J. Tinsley has argued, prophecy and poetry have always overlapped, and the area where they do so is that of mystical experience and revelation. But among many modern biblical theologians both mystical experience and its expression in allegory or myth are regarded with suspicion. Indeed much of the ineffectiveness of 'second-order' theology is due to the fact that it adopts an ostrich-like attitude to these things; burying its head in the sands of textual criticism and linguistic minutiae, it declares that, for it, mysticism and mystical allegory do not exist, and so produces elaborately intellectualized interpretations of what are in essence religious art-forms.

[1] On this, see the essay by E. J. Tinsley, 'Parable Allegory and Mysticism', in *Vindications* (S.C.M., London, 1966).

In this way theology, which starts as mystical theology, where it refers to actual religious experience, can become scholastic theology, and thus eventually scholasticism, by which time it is in danger of losing any real connection with living religion. This happens however, only where the devotional and ritual disciplines of religion are disregarded, where contemplation and meditation are rejected, where theologians come to regard theology as the primary and most essential activity and fail to respect the fact that its proper position is that of the servant and interpreter of religious experience, of that which is directly known and encountered in the holy life.

MORIBUND THEOLOGY AND LIVING RELIGION

Thus a situation can be reached where professional theology and living religion are almost completely divorced, a situation in which the unschooled but saintly believer may intuitively catch more of the meaning of those documents of mystical theology which are called the New Testament than can the most high-powered professional theological intellect; a situation where, on the other hand, the study of theology can be undertaken by the person who has no time for the life of religion. The situation is not one peculiar to Christianity, of course; it seems to have occurred wherever there has been an exclusive reliance on sacred scripture as the one medium of religious 'revelation'. This is what had happened in Judaism in the centuries immediately preceding the birth of Jesus, when the study of the Jewish Law, the Torah, had become the sole preoccupation of the scribe, the characteristic figure of Judaism. It was in some measure in protest against this that the new outburst of mystical-prophetic religion took place, which eventually became known as the Christian *ecclesia*. And when in the succeeding centuries scribalism crept back once more in the guise of scholasticism and biblicism it was always the Christian mystics and prophets, men to whom the religious life and the personal reality of God were more important than theological systems, who resisted this slow death and revitalized Christian religion. In Islam, too, when Qur'ānic orthodoxy had become a matter almost exclusively of logic and law, the influence of Sufi mysticism brought new life into Islam, through the experience of such a man as Al Ghazali, who as Professor of Theology in Baghdad in the early twelfth century, had found that theology led only to scepticism and nihilism. Turning to the writings of the mystics he began to comprehend that the truth with which theology claims to deal 'cannot be comprehended by study but only by direct ecstatic experience and after a spiritual rebirth. . . . What a difference there is', he continues, 'between the knowledge of the scientific definition of intoxication . . . and actual intoxication. I understood that mystics are men who have actual experiences, not just theories, and I realized that, as far as it was possible, I had made some progress along the road of intellectual understanding. What was left could not be achieved by studying books and by oral instruction (i.e. even in mystical religion) but only by direct experience and by following the mystic faith.'[1]

In modern times it is theology which once again has been threatening to dominate Christianity. Theology, that is, as the study of other men's study of those documents which in the first place were thrown up in the enthusiasm of spiritual experience; theology as an undertaking which is at several removes from and well insulated against the reality of which the scriptures speak; theology as an intellectual activity, characterized by reading and expounding and arguing and counter-arguing, so that for much of Christianity the authority has become the professor's gown in the pulpit or the 'open book' before the

[1] Quoted by A. Hottinger, *The Arabs* (London, 1963), p. 94.

congregation, rather than any living encounter with reality as *personal* in a sacramental community.

In view of this it is little wonder that theology ceases to be relevant to life and the adjective 'theological' is used by a British Prime Minister to mean that which is unverifiable, meaningless and irrelevant.[1]

What has happened to theology when it reaches this low level is that it has fallen a victim to the perennial danger of individualism. It has succumbed to what, in its own understanding of human existence, is the basic form of temptation, the assertion of the ultimacy of the individual human ego. And inevitably, in such a context of thought, the conception of God with which theology will concern itself will be that of *a celestial individual*. It is precisely this conception of God which leads theology into all kinds of unnecessary difficulties, and lays it open to the charge of irrelevance from its modern critics, from Feuerbach onwards. The crux of the matter then is that cerebral theology has become entirely divorced from mystical theology. Let us examine this point a little more closely, and see why it is fraught with such danger.

Individuation is an inescapable stage of human existence; it is part of the process of growing up. In what he has written concerning 'the emergence of the individual'[2] Erich Fromm points out that for a considerable period of its early life a child remains functionally one with its mother, even after becoming a biological entity separate from her. But the more the child grows, the more these primary ties are cut off as the process of individuation ensues. With this goes both a growing *self-strength*, and a growing *aloneness*. 'The primary ties offer security and basic unity with the world outside oneself. To the

[1] Harold Wilson, quoted by J. Robinson, *The New Reformation?* (1965), p. 76.

[2] Erich Fromm, *The Fear of Freedom* (1942), ch. ii.

extent to which the child emerges from that world it becomes aware of being alone, of being an entity separate from all others. This separation from a world, which in comparison with one's own individual existence is overwhelmingly strong and powerful, and often threatening and dangerous, creates a feeling of powerlessness and anxiety.'[1]

One way out of this situation is 'to give up one's individuality, to overcome the feeling of aloneness and powerlessness by completely submerging oneself in the world outside'.[2] But this creates its own problems: the child never *can* reverse the process of individuation, psychically, any more than it can physically return to its mother's womb. So the attempt to submerge oneself by complete submission to some external authority is never fully satisfactory; the result is the very opposite of what was intended; the individual remains conscious of a contradiction between the self and the authority to which it seeks to submit, and this creates insecurity, hostility and rebelliousness.

The other way out of this situation of aloneness and anxiety is that of '*spontaneous relationship to man and nature*'.[3] Thus, the growing separation involved in the process of individuation 'may result in an isolation that has the quality of desolation and creates intense anxiety and insecurity; it may result in a new kind of closeness and a solidarity with others if the child has been able to develop the inner strength and productivity which are the premiss of this new kind of relatedness to the world'.[4]

Here, in brief outline, is the situation which Marxism deals with in one way, and Buddhism and mystical theology in another. The point from which all three start is the condition of fear and anxiety felt by the self-conscious individual; in Buddhism it is the man whose life is characterized by *dukkha*; in Marxism, self-alienated man; in Christian theology, fallen man. Unless this condition is effectively dealt with it will continually

[1] Op. cit., p. 23.   [2] Ibid.   [3] Ibid., p. 24.   [4] Ibid., p. 25.

reassert itself, and so will the fear and anxiety that go with it. In each of the three ways of dealing with it that we are concerned with the solution lies in the direction of a real re-relating of the individual self to some supra-individual sphere of existence.

THE DANGER OF BIBLICISM

Theology is concerned with the re-relating of the individual to the realm of *personal* being. The context in which this takes place is religion, in this case theistic religion. The ways in which the individual finds his separateness, his egoism, transcended and taken up into a fuller life, in prayer and devotion, in communion and the life of community — all these make up religion. The purpose, the *raison d'être* of religion, at least in the Christian case, is the entry into and the maintaining of the life of true personal being.

Now what happens when religion moves its centre of gravity away from the personal being of God to *a book* is that it becomes concept-ridden and intellectualized. It has now shifted its attention away from the *personal* reality with which Christian mystical theology deals to an object, an 'it'. The leading and influential figures in the religious system then become the *biblical* and *scholastic* theologians, expounders of a text, men whose concern is cerebral rather than mystical. And in this situation religion becomes in effect a matter of performing exercises in theology; it becomes an activity which is determined not by the living reality of personal being but by the bounds of the theological system and the canon of scripture. Scripture, which was at first a witness to a living reality, is made a tyrant to which the whole life of religion has to be subjected. Everything that men seek to do in their religious life must be justified in terms of scripture, supported by reference to scripture, and may be denounced on the alleged authority of scripture. Scripture, in fact, now takes the place of God; the letter replaces the spirit; a dead thing is exalted in the place of the living and the personal. This tyranny of the book has occurred in Jewish, Christian and Muslim theology alike.

In such a situation there is now no longer any *living* check on man's innate tendency to individualism. The way out of the human state of isolated individuation, with all its dangers and anxieties, which first-order, or mystical, theology offers, is the relating of the individual, through prayer, meditation and sacrament, to the personal realm of being, to that reality which theology describes as God, the reality that is characterized as holy, transcendental, and personal. But the way out of the state of isolated individuation which second-order theology offers is, in effect, to resort to a book. Biblicists may reply that resort to a book is made because the book *alone* points the way to the experience of the knowledge of God. But in effect the book is made the arbiter of religious experience; and, what is more damaging, this or that biblical theologian's *interpretation* of the book is made the arbiter. The view of mystical theology on the other hand is that scripture (i.e. first-order theological writings, Jewish, Christian or Muslim) may confirm and corroborate the knowledge of the living God which man has in living the religious life. The view of biblical theology is that scripture tells man what he needs to know of God, which he himself may then *possibly* find confirmed in his religious life. This is the cerebral approach to religion; it makes intellectual agreement with certain formal doctrines (derived from this or that scribe's exposition of such religious writings as have been canonized) the fundamental and primary feature, to which everything else in the religion is subordinate and to which everything else must conform; and this kind of approach may render religion incapable of performing its most important function in human life. It reflects a view of man in which he consists principally of a mind, a being whose chief activity is discursive thought. In this view man is regarded as controlling himself by his self-conscious thoughts. It is a view which ignores altogether the areas of a man's life which are not subject to the individual's cogitation, areas where he is motivated by forces and pressures in his own nature and in his society of which he may be only dimly aware, or even totally unaware.

It is this kind of approach which has been characteristic of a great deal of Western religion in modern times; the virtual ineffectiveness of religion to deal with the human condition might be said to be in direct relation to the degree to which religion is under the dominance of 'second-order' theology.

By its ineffectiveness to deal with the human condition is meant, primarily, the condition already described, in which man's development necessarily involves individuation, a condition which brings fears and anxieties, a condition from which he must be delivered by being re-related to some supra-individual order of being. To relate man to the personal being of God is the function of theistic religion, but when the vitality of religion has been drained away by theology, man is left in his state of painful and unredeemed individuation. He is left in the position of Descartes where the only statement he can make that appears to him to have any validity is that he thinks, therefore he exists — and from this he passes easily to the view that the ultimate and final reality is an individual mind, engaged in lonely cogitation. This then is how he understands the concept God; his own unrelieved individuation is projected upon the heavens, he makes God in his own individualistic image; for the Western man who has been offered only theology when his need was for religion God thus becomes a celestial individual, 'out there,' thinking his vast, lonely thoughts. In this Feuerbach was right; right in his analysis, and right to criticize the theology that had led European man into this situation. 'Theology is pathology hidden from itself.'[1]

Feuerbach was aware that the theology of his day had served man ill. He was concerned moreover, for those values which it seemed to him theology had betrayed, the predicates of the Divine Being which this image of God as a celestial individual destroyed. Theology had effectively disguised the reality of religion; Christianity had become, said Feuerbach, no more than an *idée fixe*; an idea which was repudiated by the facts of European life: 'it is in flagrant contradiction with our Fire and Life Assurance companies, our railroads and steam carriages, our picture and sculpture galleries, our military and industrial schools, our theatres and scientific museums.'[2]

This is a pertinent criticism of a great deal of theology still. It is almost a truism to say that most of the trouble in which theology finds itself today is due to the fact that it is, by its own deliberate choice, out of touch with the brute realities of contemporary existence. In some universities in England it is possible for an undergraduate to study theology without ever having to concern himself with anything later than the fourth century A.D. It is not surprising that such an activity is dismissed by many as an irrelevance, and tolerated by others purely for its archaeological interest. It is not surprising also that Western, especially Protestant, society in Europe and America is characterized by individualism. True personal being, the life of human beings in community, has to yield place almost everywhere to the autonomy of the individual. This is to be observed in various spheres of activity but perhaps nowhere more clearly than in Protestant religion.

Whether this situation can be attributed, even partly at least,

[1] *Werke*, vi. 107, quoted by Acton, op. cit., p. 121.
[2] *The Essence of Christianity*, trans. by George Eliot (Harper, New York, 1957), p. xliv.

to the effects of Western theology is a difficult question to decide. Some Christians would say that the theological tradition of the West must bear part of the blame for the disease of individualism which in the West inhibits an authentic social doctrine.[1] Certainly, in this situation second-order theology can contribute nothing towards remedying the chaotic state of human affairs. When and where men become aware of the need for some more positive view of human existence, for wholeness and coherence, it is not to theology *as it is commonly taught* and understood that they will turn.

It would be a great mistake, however, if in the twentieth century men were to reject religion along with traditional theology. For religion — if by this we mean the ways in which man is related to transcendental holy, personal, reality — is not dependent on theology. Theology is religion's servant; when theology assumes the position of the master of religion it does so as a usurper. In the West, second-order theology, thus dominating religion, has resulted in second-order religion. It is no wonder that some have conceived the notion of religionless Christianity. Or to put it another way it is no wonder that because theology seemed to control religion and theology seemed largely irrelevant that religion should have come to seem irrelevant also. But what we have tried to show here is that this is a false analysis.

To say this is not to subscribe to the view that 'God is no more',[2] or that God died, and died in our time. The only god who is dead is the god of a great deal of contemporary theology. And this is because such theology has lost any real contact with the sacred.[3] It may be difficult for modern men to believe in the god of scholasticism, the god of the classical arguments, but this

[1] See K. Leech, in *Theology* (March 1965), p. 139.
[2] See the book by this title by Werner Pelz.
[3] T. J. J. Altizer, *Mircea Eliade and the Dialectic of the Sacred* (1963), p. 14.

is because, as Kierkegaard found, the god of the philosophers is not the God of Abraham, Isaac and Jacob. The real difficulty in belief in God is that orthodox theology, which has been engaged for so long in regurgitating what *others* have said about God, has now arrived at the stage where the last faint trace of a living sense of the sacred has been processed out of existence. Nowhere is this more plainly seen than in the contemporary Protestant claim that faith in God is directed *against* religion; it is here indeed that the contemporary neo-orthodoxy reveals its own alienation from the sacred.[1]

Theology may be the sick man of Europe today, even supposing that in its classical forms it is not already dead; but it would be a mistake to think that because traditional theology is about to expire, religion is going to die with it.

[1] Altizer, op. cit., p. 14.

14

RELIGION IN THE
MODERN WORLD

THE SOCIOLOGICAL APPRECIATION
OF RELIGION

I T is a curious fact that while neo-orthodox Christian
theologians are today busy denouncing religion, professional
anthropologists and sociologists are pointing out its value, and
the important place it has in human society. Kingsley Davis's
words may be taken as a representative example: 'Since every
society seems to have something called religion, its presence can
hardly be dismissed as a sociological accident. If, given the
major conditions of human social life as known up to now,
religion made no contribution to societal survival or was not
inextricably attached to something that did contribute to
survival, one would expect that social systems and cultures
would long since have evolved without it.'[1] He goes on to
point out that the importance of religion is seen best when its
place in society is examined in relation to other major structures
— economic, political or familial, for instance. 'If in the face of
the other major structures religion retains a separate place, being
no more dependent on them than they are on it, the argument

[1] Introduction to *Religion Among the Primitives*, by W. J. Goode (1951),
p. 15.

206

for its functional role in the social system is hard to deny.'[1]

Perhaps the most notable name in this connection is that of Talcott Parsons, whose work in the field of the sociology of religion, following upon the theories of Weber, Durkheim, and Malinowski, has been particularly concerned with defining the role of religion in human society, and the important function which it performs, which Parsons would regard as a necessary function, so that where no religion in the sense of a pattern of practices, beliefs and institutions reflecting men's sense of the sacred is present, some *functional* alternative will have to take its place.[2]

Thus, as we have seen, while Marxist Communism cannot be regarded in the strict sense as a religion, in the situation in Russia in which Christian traditional religion is rejected by the Communist Party the need for a functional alternative shows itself in the way that Communism assumes some of the forms and functions of a religion. In the view of religion adopted by some sociologists Communism would come very close indeed to being a religion. Gerhard Lenski, for example, defines religion as 'a system of beliefs about the nature of the force(s) ultimately shaping man's destiny, and the practices associated therewith, shared by the members of a group'.[3] Thus defined, the word religion will include theistic and non-theistic faiths, even Communism, and, as Lenski points out, given this definition it is inevitable that religion must be regarded as universal. However, the definition is now probably so wide that it fails to be of much value in identifying religion and bringing

[1] Op. cit., p. 17.

[2] For a brief general account of Talcott Parson's work in this connection see 'Religious Perspectives in Sociology and Social Psychology', in *Reader in Comparative Religion*, ed. by W. A. Lessa and E. Z. Vogt (Evanston and New York, 1958).

[3] G. Lenski, *The Religious Factor: A Sociologist's Enquiry* (Anchor Books, 1963), p. 331.

out its singular importance in human life. In particular what this definition lacks is a reference to *the sense of the sacred* which both distinguishes such systems as Hinduism, Buddhism, Islam and Christianity from Communism and humanism, and also is the secret of the enduring nature of religion. It is this which guarantees for religion a continuing place in human affairs. And it is with religion in this sense that we have been concerned in this book. It will be useful at this point briefly to make some observations about the nature of religion which emerge from our study, and then to point out some of the implications of what we have seen to be religion's special status in human society.

THE PRACTICAL FUNCTIONS OF RELIGION

First, religion always implies *action* of some kind. 'Religion, according to the savage, is essentially something you do,' wrote R. R. Marett,[1] and this holds good for religion at more sophisticated levels. The Buddhist monk at his meditation may appear entirely inactive; but in fact he is intensely active in the work of concentration, only the action is inward rather than outward. In the case of other developed religions it is hardly necessary to comment. The prayer-ritual of the Muslim performed five times a day, and the life lived in obedience to the precepts of Islam; the eucharistic liturgy of the Christian and the sacramental common life which undergirds it and of which it is the expression; these also are essentially actions — actions of the whole man, bodily, mental and spiritual. The root meaning of the word 'liturgy' serves to emphasize this: it is the 'people's work', that which is done by the whole people.

[1] *Faith, Hope, and Charity in Primitive Religion*, p. 11. See also W. J. Goode, *Religion Among the Primitives*, pp. 221 f.: 'Religion is action, not merely a set of philosophic speculations about another world.'

Secondly, what is done has *significance*. A meaning has been perceived, in the world and in human existence, and the way a man relates his own life or the life of his people to this meaning is religion. Men do not sit down and work out life's meaning, and then set about performing ritual actions that demonstrate or reflect this meaning. In life and in history the processes of religion are more complicated than that. The first religious action of man, whatever that may have been, may very well have been performed with only the dimmest awareness on man's part of why he was performing this, or precisely *how* it was related to the sense of the holy, or of the eternal, or the terribly powerful. Religious action may well have been in origin almost instinctive. What distinguishes religious actions from others of a similar nature which are not religious is that the religious action embodies a *meaning*, and it implies some kind of an evaluation of what is of supreme worth within the whole scheme of things. Thus when man has ceased to hold any such evaluation of existence, when there is no longer anything that has for him ultimate value, *then* he may really be said to have ceased to be religious.

The claim that is made by some scientific humanists that science can and does supply human life with meaning thus qualifies scientific humanism to be regarded as a religion, or at least a quasi-religion. It is not fully a religion, for it is lacking in specific ritual actions by means of which the meaning which has been perceived is made relevant to everyday life here and now. It is worth noting that this is what Sir Julian Huxley considers to be humanism's need today: 'We shall need . . . a new religious terminology, and a re-formulation of religious concepts in a new idiom. A humanist religion will have to work out its own rituals and its own basic symbolism.'[1] The same is true of Communism, although in some places Com-

---

[1] *The Observer*, Sunday, 31 March 1963.

munism verges already on becoming a religion in the full sense, where, as in Germany recently, it attempts to introduce such elements as initiation rites. But in this particular case it is more probable that Communism is simply imitating the Catholic Church for special reasons of its own, namely in order to detach young people from the Church and redirect their allegiance. The ritual does not proceed naturally from the nature of Communism, which elsewhere exists without such rituals. Nevertheless, the fact that the tendency does show itself is significant, for it suggests that, the nature of man being what it is, there is always an inclination for a quasi-religion to become religious in the full sense.

The third observation to be made about religion concerns its *comprehensiveness*. It might even be described as totalitarian, in so far as it permits no rival loyalties, and because it takes all aspects of human life within its scope. The Buddhist monk does not regard his religion as one compartment of life alongside others. It overarches all he does, even the most commonplace activities — how he sits and how he stands, how he walks and how he lies down to sleep; he does all these things, as he would say, 'mindfully'; he does them as a Buddhist. The precepts contained in the *Vinaya*, the code of laws governing the life of the monks, appear to cater for every conceivable contingency of life. The same is true of the Muslim. Consciousness of his membership of the community of Islam colours all his activities in the world, including for example, as we are being made very much aware today in the Middle East and elsewhere, political life and action. The same is true again of Hinduism: the way the Hindu brushes his teeth and bathes himself on rising, even the way he cooks his food, or uses the privy — all these activities are regulated for him in the household laws of Hinduism. So closely interwoven for the Hindu are mythology and prayer and sacrifice with all the commonplace things of life that one is justified in saying that Hinduism is a culture and a religion at the same time, or that religion and life are synonymous. In Christian tradition the intention is the same. The comprehensiveness of Christianity is expressed by St. Cyril of Jerusalem's words concerning the catholicity of the Church: 'It is called Catholic because it extends through the whole world from one end to the other; and because it teaches with wholeness and without defect all the truths that men need to know, of things seen and unseen, of things heavenly and earthly; and because it disciplines unto holiness every sort of men, rulers and subjects, educated and ignorant. . . .'[1]

This comprehensiveness of religion, this characteristic of developed religion in bringing all life within its scope, in Buddhism, Islam, and Christianity, in Hinduism and, one might add, in Judaism, indicates moreover that there is an awareness in all these faiths that holiness has other contexts besides that of the sanctuary. Norman Pittenger has called these other contexts the secular 'incognitos' of God.[2] An awareness of God's presence and reality may take hold of the Christian, for example, as he contemplates the beauty of nature, or of great art, or as he engages in scientific research, or studies history, or in various other outwardly 'secular' ways. To be reminded of this fact is a valuable corrective against narrow religiosity.

The fourth general observation that must be made is that in addition to gathering together into itself all the many different activities of life, religion does something more: it brings all these activities into focus. That is to say, religion relates the mundane affairs of life to the meaning that has been perceived in life as a whole, and it does this through certain characteristic activities of religion. These are the ways in which religion persists separately from politics and economics, referred to by

---

[1] St. Cyril, *Catecheses*, xviii. 23.
[2] *Theology* (Feb. 1962), pp. 45 ff.

Kingsley Davis. The secular 'incognitos' which have just been mentioned do not provide man with the fullest possible knowledge of the Holy that is available to him. A more direct confrontation is the essence and core of all the great religions. This is as fully true in Buddhism as in any other faith, even though there is in this system no conception of God. For while, in Buddhism as in other religions, all life comes within the purview of Buddhist morality, and every action in life is a potential opportunity for influencing one's future *karma*, it is acknowledged that there are certain special patterns of activity in the performance of which men draw nearer to the Holy.

It is in the special activity of disciplined meditation that the Buddhist reaches the heart of his religion, and enters the 'stream' of salvation, on the far side of which he will find transcendental wisdom. The activity of meditation, according to the principles and special insights of Buddhism, is the focus of the whole of the Buddhist way of life; it is significant that an alternative name for it is 'concentration', the bringing of everything to a single point, and it is in this way that enlightenment will eventually be reached.

For the Christian the ritual activity in which all life's common activities find their focus is the Holy Eucharist. Here supremely is the place where man's previous encounters with God *incognito* in the life of the world are related to the knowledge of God as he has been revealed in Christ. It is here that all the latent religious experience which has been gained in secular contexts will be rendered significant and filled with meaning. While in the broad sense all life is sacramental, there is for Christians an acknowledged centre for sacramental living, a centre where it is all held together and given profound significance.

The Eucharist, of all the activities in which a Christian engages, is, essentially, religious activity. Professor Guillaume, in his great work on Hebrew prophecy,[1] points to the Eucharist as the culminating *act* of the whole Hebrew prophetic tradition, and thus, in a sense, of Hebrew religion. Charles Gore saw in it, he said, the realization of all that the untaught or half-taught religious instincts of man had been feeling after in every part of the world. The *focus* of the Christian faith is to be found in this, its most characteristically *religious*, activity.

So it is in each of the great religions: the focal point is found in the kind of activity that is commonly thought of as 'religious' (that is, connected with the sanctuary) and it is usually this activity of the sanctuary which is seized upon and attacked by those who are critical of 'religion'. The activity of the sanctuary is so peculiarly the characteristic of religion that in course of time it comes to be regarded as *the whole* of religion; religion is thought of as consisting of this, *and this only*. But the truth is that while the activity of the sanctuary is certainly the essence and heart of religion, nevertheless it loses all its significance and value if it is cut off from its roots in the common life of men. For the Buddhist there can be no genuine meditation that is not firmly based upon and supported by moral living at the every-day level. Morality, in all the common affairs of life, is the plant on which alone meditation can bloom. The blossom will soon wither if it is severed from the plant that sustains it.

Much of the current confusion in discussions about religion-less faith arises from this mistaken view, in which religion is seen as an affair of *the sanctuary only*, and not as a total way of life. The matter is complicated by the fact that in the West many of the adherents of religion have themselves fallen into the same error. Once religion is cut down in this way and reduced to certain special activities which are unrelated to the rest of life, it very easily becomes *religiosity*, and as such deserves to be rejected.

This leads to the fifth general observation: religious systems

[1] *Prophecy and Divination* (1938), p. 367.

of all kinds exhibit a recurring tendency to settle down into *legalism*. Consider, for example, what a Buddhist monk from North India has written about the Buddhism of South-East Asia: 'Rigid observance of the strict letter of the Vinaya, at least while under public surveillance, is all that is expected of the monk in most parts of the so-called Theravada world today. In most cases the monk accepts the role allotted to him by society, and plays it extremely well, with the result that the Theravada Sangha has become a veritable hothouse for hypocrisy in all its most orchidaceous varieties. Exquisite and extraordinary blossoms of monastic formalism which, parasitic upon the mighty trunk of the Dharma, suck from it all vitality and strength, can be gathered by the basketful by any observant pilgrim to the home, or rather homes, of "pure Buddhism".'[1] The severity of the judgement which this monk makes on his co-religionists is to some extent to be explained, no doubt, as a reflection of the controversy between the two varieties of Buddhism, the Mahayana and the Theravada; a good deal could be said to mitigate the harshness of his words. But no one who knows anything of the Buddhism of South-East Asia would deny that there is some truth in what he says.

The same kind of deterioration has occurred at various times in the history of all the great religions. The history of Islam in the early nineteenth century is marked by the formation of a number of puritan reformist movements, aimed at recovering the original purity of Islam.[2] Christian history is similarly characterized by lapses into legalism and corruption, and the ensuing movements of reform. It seems that in every religion there occur periods when religious vitality is low, or when a kind of hardening of the arteries sets in, and the reality of the faith is obscured by formalism. The ability to recover from such

---

[1] Bhikshu Sangharakshita, *A Survey of Buddhism* (1959), p. 239.
[2] See, for example, H. A. R. Gibb, *Mohammedanism* (1949), pp. 170 ff.

periods of *malaise* depends in each case on the structure and the make-up of the religion concerned: some seem better able to recover than others. But while in the history of every religion we can observe such instances of religion-gone-to-seed, they must not be taken to be characteristic and representative specimens of religion *per se*. We must not fall into the error of supposing that because we reject corrupt religion (as we should) we are rejecting religion itself. Men do not give up eating eggs just because some eggs are sometimes found to be bad.

The error involved in rejecting 'religion' out of hand, because of its corruptions, becomes most apparent in the light of the last and most important aspect of religion to be mentioned here, namely that religion is *response*. We may recall the words of Archbishop William Temple: 'All that is noble in the non-Christian systems of thought, or conduct, or worship is the work of Christ upon them and within them. By the Word of God — that is to say, by Jesus Christ — Isaiah and Plato, and Zoroaster, and Buddha, and Confucius conceived and uttered such truths as they declared. There is only one divine light; and every man in his measure is enlightened by it.'[1]

RELIGION, GOD, AND SOCIETY

To see religion as a necessary, special kind of response which men make out of an awareness of an 'entirely other which is over against us', means that *religion*, far from needing to be despised after the fashion of some theologians, is an activity to be respected and honoured. The glory of religion is a reflected glory, a reflection in some measure of the one divine light, the transcendental holy. It is religiosity which is the distorting element in religion, the element that has to be guarded against, but it is most important that we should not mistake this for

[1] *Readings in St. John's Gospel* (1945), p. 10.

religion itself. For a deeper understanding of religion will help us to see its noble potentialities for the future of man and how impoverished human existence would be without it.

There are thus two ways of understanding and appreciating religion. One is the theological approach; the other is the sociological. It will be clear that the theological understanding of religion belongs to 'first-order' or mystical theology and not to the theology of the scribes. It is an appreciation of religion as the highest of all man's activity, that in which he draws nearest to reality, and approaches the highest reaches of true person-hood, a sacramental activity to which the service of his fellow-men, morality, art, literature and science are all contributory. In Christian terms this is the way to the knowledge of God, in Buddhist terms, to Enlightenment.

In contrast with this the sociological appreciation of religion may seem banal. But it has an importance which has not yet been widely recognized by professional theologians. For from this point of view religion is seen as a perennial and ineradicable feature of human life. In the sociologist's view it is unlikely to disappear so long as human society lasts. Science is not in competition with religion, though it may, rightly, prove hostile to a dead theology, and it may have the effect therefore of inhibiting a religion which is closely tied to an irrelevant or dead theology. Even the most recently industrialized societies, where the advance of technology has been greatest, show no signs of the withering away of religion, confidently predicted by nineteenth-century rationalists. In the Western world the United States, and in the Eastern world Japan both present evidence of the luxuriant growths which religion can produce in a highly complex technological society.[1]

[1] See, for example, H. J. Thomsen, *The New Religions of Japan* (Rutland, Vermont, and Tokyo, 1963); B. R. Wilson, *Sects and Society* (London, 1961); and Gerhard Lenski, *The Religious Factor* (New York, 1961).

The sociologist's concern (*qua* sociologist) is with the persistence and vitality and social function of religion, especially at those points where it affects and is affected by other human activities, economic, political and so on. But the substance and content and sources of the religious life in the modern world are the proper concern of theologians — if by this is meant those who understand and know, if only a little, something of the profound and rich potentialities for human existence which religion possesses, those who know from within something of the meaning and the value of the religious life.

BIBLIOGRAPHY

Note: This selected bibliography is restricted to books and articles made use of and referred to in the present work.

A. BUDDHISM — GENERAL

Anon., *The Betrayal of Buddhism*. Balangoda, 1956.

Bapat, P. V. (ed.), *2,500 Years of Buddhism*. Delhi, 1956.

Bigandet, P., *The Life, or Legend of Gaudama The Buddha of the Burmese*. Rangoon 1866.

Chattopadhyaya, D., *Lokayata: A Study in Ancient Indian Materialism*. New Delhi, 1959.

Conze, E., *A Short History of Buddhism*. Bombay, 1960.

— *Buddhist Meditation*. London, 1956.

— *Buddhist Thought in India*. London, 1962.

de Lubac, H., *Aspects of Buddhism* (trans. by George Lamb). New York, 1954.

— *Le Rencontre du Bouddhisme et de l'Occident*. Paris, 1952.

Dutt, S., *Early Buddhist Monachism*. London, 1924.

— *Buddhist Monks and Monasteries of India*. London, 1962.

Eliot, C. H., *Hinduism and Buddhism* (3 vols.). London, 1921.

Hackmann, H., *Buddhism as a Religion*. London, 1910.

Ling, T. O., *Buddhism and the Mythology of Evil*. London, 1962.

— 'Buddhist Mysticism' in *Religious Studies* (Cambridge), vol. i, no. 2.

Malalasekera, G. P., 'The East and West and Buddhism', in *The Middle Way*, vol. xxxiii, no. 4.

Mus, P., 'Bouddhisme et monde occidentale par une nouvelle méthod' in *Présence du Bouddhism*. Saigon, 1959.

Murti, T. R. V., *The Central Philosophy of Buddhism*. London, 1955.

Nyanaponika, *Abhidhamma Studies*. Colombo, 1949.

— *The Heart of Buddhist Meditation*. Colombo, 1956.

Nyanatiloka, *Guide Through the Abhidhamma Pitaka*. Colombo, 1957.

Bibliography

Pratt, J. B., *The Pilgrimage of Buddhism*. London, 1928.

Ray, N. R., *Theravada Buddhism in Burma*. Calcutta, 1946.

Saddhatissa, H., *Handbook of Buddhists*. Banaras, 1956.

Sangharakshita, *A Survey of Buddhism*. 2nd edn., Bangalore, 1959.

Snellgrove, D., 'Buddhist Morality', in *The Springs of Morality*, ed. J. M. Todd. London, 1956.

Wells, K. E., *Thai Buddhism: Its Rites and Activities*. Bangkok, 1960.

B. CONTEMPORARY SOUTH-EAST ASIA

Anon., *The System of Correlation of Man and His Environment* (The Philosophy of the Burma Socialist Programme Party), Rangoon, 1963.

Anon., 'Nationalism in Burma', *The Times* (London, 13 Feb. 1964).

Adloff, R., and Thompson, V., *The Left Wing in Southeast Asia*. New York, 1950.

Badgley, J. H., 'Burma: the nexus of Socialism and two political traditions', in *Asian Survey*, Feb. 1963.

— 'Burma's Zealot Wungyis: Maoists or St. Simonists?', in *Asian Survey*, vol. v. no. 1 (Jan. 1965).

Ba Swe., *The Burmese Revolution*. Rangoon, 1952.

Butwell, R., *U Nu of Burma*. Stanford, California, 1963.

Carver, G. A., 'The Real Revolution in South Vietnam', in *Foreign Affairs*, Apr. 1965.

Crozier, B., 'The Communist Struggle for power in Burma', in *The World Today*, Mar. 1964.

— *South-East Asia in Turmoil*. London, 1965.

Fairburn, G., 'Aspects of the Burmese Political Scene', in *Pacific Affairs*, vol. 29. (1956).

Hall, H. Fielding, *The Soul of a People*. London, 1904.

Hobbs, Cecil, 'The Political Importance of the Buddhist Priesthood in Burma', *Far Eastern Economic Review*, xxi, (8 Nov. 1956), pp. 586–90.

Mecklin, J., *Mission in Torment* (especially ch. 5, 'The Buddhist Flash Fire'). New York, 1965.

Mendelson, E. M., 'Buddhism and the Burmese Establishment', in *Archives de Sociologie des Religions*, no. 17, 1964.

Mya Maung: 'Cultural Values and Economic Change in Burma', in *Asian Survey*, Mar. 1964.

— 'Socialism and Economic Development of Burma', in *Asian Survey*, Dec. 1964.

Nash, M., 'Southeast Asian Society', in *Journal of Asian Studies*, May 1964.

Rose, S., *Socialism in Southern Asia*. Oxford, 1959.

Scigliano, R., 'Vietnam: Politics and Religion', in *Asian Survey*, Jan. 1964.

Scott, J. G., *The Burman*. London, 1882. (Useful as background to the modern period.)

Stackelberg, G. A. von, 'U Nu and Burma', *Bulletin of the Institute for the Study of the USSR* (Munich), vol iii, no. 4, April 1956.

Tinker, H., *The Union of Burma*., 3rd edn. London, 1961.

Warner, D., *The Last Confucian* (especially ch. 13). London, 1964.

Wriggins, W. H., *Ceylon: Dilemmas of a New Nation*. Princeton, 1960.

C. MARXISM, RUSSIA AND RELIGION

Acton, H. B., *The Illusion of an Epoch*. London, 1955.

Berdyaev, N., *The Russian Revolution*. London, 1933.

Berlin, I., *Karl Marx: His Life and Environment*. 3rd edn. London, 1963.

Bottomore, T. B.: *Karl Marx: Selected Writings in Sociology and Social Philosophy*. London, 1963.

Conze, E., 'Buddhism in the Soviet Union', in *The Middle Way*, vol. xxxv, no. 3.

Engels, F., *Dialectics of Nature*. London, edition of 1955.

Florinsky, M. T., *Russia: A History and An Interpretation*. New York, 1959.

Keep, J. L. H., *The Rise of Social Democracy in Russia*. Oxford, 1963.

Kochan, L., *The Making of Modern Russia*. London, 1962.

Kolarz, W., *Religion in the Soviet Union*. London, 1961.

— *Communism and Colonialism*. London, 1964.

Lenin, V. I., *On Religion*. London, n.d.

Marx, K., *Capital*, trans. E. and C. Paul, London, 1928.

— *Economic and Philosophic Manuscripts of 1844*. Translated by M. Milligan. Moscow, 1959.

K. Marx and F. Engels, On Britain. Foreign Languages Publishing House, Moscow, 1953.

Marx, K., and Engels, F., *On Religion*. Moscow, n.d.

Milligan, M. 'Marxism and Morality', in *Marxism Today*, vol. ix, no. 1 (Jan. 1965).

Monnerot, J., *Sociology of Communism*. London, 1953.

Pares, B., *A History of Russia*. London, 1947.

Paskiewicz, H., *The Making of the Russian Nation*. London, 1963.

Plamenatz, J., *German Marxism and Russian Communism*. London, 1954.

Bibliography

Poppe, N., 'The Destruction of Buddhism in the USSR', in *Bulletin of the Institute for the Study of the USSR*, July 1956.

Russell, B., *A History of Western Philosophy*. London, 1946.

Trager, F. N. (ed.), *Marxism in Southeast Asia*. Stanford, California, 1960.

Tucker, R., *Philosophy and Myth in Karl Marx*. Cambridge, 1961.

Ulam, A. B., *The Unfinished Revolution*. New York, 1960.

Zernov, N., *Eastern Christendom*. London, 1961.

D. CHINA, JAPAN AND TIBET

Ch'en, J. 'China's Conception of her Place in the World', *Political Quarterly*, vol. xxxv no. 3 (1964).

Dawson, R. (ed.), *The Legacy of China*. Oxford, 1964.

Fitzgerald, C. P., *Flood Tide in China*. London, 1958.

— *The Chinese View of Their Place in the World*. London, 1964.

Jacobs, D. N., and Baerwald, H. H. (eds.), *Chinese Communism: Selected Documents*. New York, 1963.

Lamb, A., *The China–India Border* (Chatham House Essays no. 2). Oxford, 1965.

Lee, W., 'General Aspects of Chinese Communist Religious Policy, with Soviet Comparisons', in *China Quarterly*, July–Sept. 1964.

Maki, J. M., *Government and Politics in Japan*. London, 1962.

Migot, A., 'Le Bouddhisme en Chine', in *Présence du Bouddhisme*, Saigon, 1959.

Robinson, R. H., 'Buddhism in China and Japan', in *The Concise Encyclopaedia of Living Faiths*, ed. R. C. Zaehner. London, 1959.

Richardson, H. E., *Tibet and Its History*. London, 1962.

Rupen, R. A., 'Inside Outer Mongolia', in *Foreign Affairs*, vol. 37, no. 2, Jan. 1959.

Thomsen, H. J., *The New Religions of Japan*. Rutland, Vermont, and Tokyo, 1963.

Welch, H., 'Buddhism Under the Communists', in *China Quarterly*, June 1961.

— 'The Chinese Sangha', in *Buddhist Annual*. Colombo, 1964.

Wright, A. F., *Buddhism in Chinese History*. Stanford, California, 1959.

Yang, C. K., *Religion in Chinese Society*. California, 1961.

E. WESTERN THEOLOGY

Altizer, T. J. J., *Mircea Eliade and the Dialectic of the Sacred*. Philadelphia, 1963.

Barth, K., *Church Dogmatics*. Edinburgh. 12 vols., 1957–63.

— *Against the Stream.* London, 1945.

Caldin, E. F., 'A Scientist's Approach to Morality', in *The Springs of Morality*, ed. J. M. Todd. London, 1956.

Coulson, J. (ed.), *Theology and the University.* London, 1964.

Feuerbach, L., *The Essence of Christianity*, trans. by George Eliot, with an introduction by Karl Barth. New York, 1957.

Heim, K., *Christian Faith and Natural Science.* London, 1953.

Hepburn, R., *et al., Religion and Humanism.* London, 1964.

Jenkins, D., *Beyond Religion.* London, 1962.

Macmurray, J., *Persons in Relation.* London, 1961.

Pettinger, W. N., 'Secular Study and Christian Faith', in *Theology*, Feb. 1962.

Polanyi, M., *Personal Knowledge.* London, 1958.

— 'Faith and Reason', in *The Journal of Religion*, Oct. 1961.

Tennant, F. R., *Philosophical Theology.* Cambridge, 1930.

Tillich, P., *Dynamics of Faith.* London, 1957.

Tinsley, E. J., 'Parable, Allegory and Mysticism', in *Affirmations* (ed. Hanson, A. P. C.). London, 1966.

Webb, C. C. J., *God and Personality.* London, 1918.

Williams, H. A., 'Theology and Self Awareness', in *Soundings*, (ed. A. R. Vidler). Cambridge, 1963.

F. SOCIOLOGY AND RELIGION

Fromm, E., *The Fear of Freedom.* London, 1942.

— *The Sane Society.* London, 1956.

Goode, W. J., *Religion Among the Primitives.* New York, 1951.

Lenski, G., *The Religious Factor: A Sociologist's Enquiry.* New York, 1961.

McClelland, D. C., *The Achieving Society.* Princeton, 1961.

Parsons, Talcott, 'Religious Perspectives in Sociology and Social Psychology', in *Reader in Comparative Religion* (ed. Lessa, W. A., and Vogt, E. Z.). New York, 1963.

Tawney, R. H., *Religion and the Rise of Capitalism.* London, 1926.

Weber, Max, *The Protestant Ethic and the Spirit of Capitalism.* Trans. Talcott Parsons. London, 1930.

Wilson, B. R., *Sects and Society.* London, 1961.

Yinger, J. M., *Religion, Society and the Individual.* New York, 1957.

INDEX

Note: Names printed in capitals are those of modern authors.

223